Hands-On Python and

From Basics to Real-World Applications

Sarful Hassan

Table of Contents

Chapter 1: Introduction to Python and NumPy

What is Python?

Python is a high-level, interpreted programming language known for its simplicity and readability. Developed by Guido van Rossum and released in 1991, Python has grown into one of the most popular programming languages today, widely used in web development, data analysis, artificial intelligence, scientific computing, and more. Its versatile syntax and active community make it a great choice for both beginners and experienced programmers.

Key features of Python:

- **Readable and simple syntax**: Python's syntax is straightforward, reducing the learning curve for beginners.
- **Dynamic typing**: Python doesn't require specifying the type of a variable. It is determined at runtime.
- **Interpreted language**: Python code is executed line by line, which makes it easier to debug.
- **Large Standard Library**: Python includes a wide range of modules and packages to handle various tasks.
- **Object-oriented**: Python supports classes and objects, which helps in organizing code efficiently.

Python's popularity is driven by:

- Its simplicity and ease of learning.
- A rich ecosystem of libraries and frameworks.
- Its ability to be used in different domains like web development (Django, Flask), data science (Pandas, NumPy), and machine learning (TensorFlow, PyTorch).

Why Python for Data Science?

Python's flexibility, combined with libraries such as NumPy, pandas, and Matplotlib, makes it one of the most powerful tools for data science. The language allows you to:

- Process and analyze large datasets efficiently.
- Perform statistical modeling.
- Visualize data in interactive plots.
- Work with machine learning algorithms.

Python also integrates well with other tools commonly used in data science, like Jupyter notebooks and SQL databases, making it an excellent choice for professionals in this field.

What is NumPy?

NumPy, short for Numerical Python, is one of the most important libraries in Python for numerical and scientific computing. It provides support for multi-dimensional arrays and matrices, along with a collection of mathematical functions to operate on these arrays. NumPy is particularly useful when working with large datasets, as it provides significant performance improvements over traditional Python lists.

Key features of NumPy:

- **N-dimensional array object (ndarray)**: The core of NumPy is its ndarray object, which allows for efficient storage and manipulation of large datasets.
- **Broadcasting**: NumPy can perform operations on arrays of different shapes in a way that simplifies code and improves performance.
- **Mathematical operations**: NumPy offers a wide range of functions for linear algebra, statistics, Fourier transforms, and random number generation.
- **Integration with C/C++/Fortran**: NumPy is built with performance in mind and can interface seamlessly with low-level languages,

allowing it to be used in high-performance computing.

Installing Python and NumPy

To get started with Python and NumPy, you need to install Python on your system along with the NumPy library. The installation process varies depending on the operating system you're using. Below are the detailed instructions for **Windows**, **Linux**, and **Mac**.

Installing Python on Windows

1. **Download Python**:
   a. Visit the official Python website.
   b. Download the latest stable version of Python for Windows.
2. **Run the Installer**:
   a. Launch the downloaded .exe file.
   b. In the installer, make sure to check the box that says **Add Python to PATH**.
   c. Click **Install Now** and follow the instructions to complete the installation.
3. **Verify Installation**:
   a. Open the **Command Prompt** (cmd) and type:

```
python --version
```
If Python is installed correctly, you should see the version number.

Installing Python on Linux

1. **Install Python**: Most Linux distributions come with Python pre-installed. However, if it's not installed, you can install it using your package manager.
   a. For **Ubuntu/Debian** based distributions:

```
sudo apt update
sudo apt install python3
```

   b. For **Fedora**:

```
sudo dnf install python3
```

2. **Verify Installation**: Open the terminal and type:

```
python3 --version
```

This should return the Python version if it's installed correctly.

Installing Python on Mac

1. **Download Python**:
   a. Visit the official Python website.
   b. Download the latest stable version of Python for Mac.
2. **Run the Installer**:
   a. Launch the .pkg installer and follow the on-screen instructions to complete the installation.
3. **Verify Installation**: Open the **Terminal** and type:

```
python3 --version
```

This will confirm that Python is installed correctly.

Installing NumPy

Once Python is installed, the next step is to install the NumPy library. You can use Python's package manager, **pip**, to install NumPy on any operating system.

1. **Open your terminal (or command prompt)** and run the following command:

```
pip install numpy
```

If you're using **Python 3**, and pip is not mapped to the Python 3 version, use pip3 instead:

```
pip3 install numpy
```

2. **Verify Installation**: To check if NumPy was installed correctly, open a Python shell by typing python or python3 in your terminal and then type:

```
import numpy as np
print(np.__version__)
```

If NumPy is installed correctly, this will display the version number of NumPy.

Alternative Installation via Anaconda

For users who prefer an all-in-one package for scientific computing, **Anaconda** is a popular Python distribution that comes pre-installed with NumPy and many other useful libraries.

1. **Download Anaconda**:
   a. Visit the Anaconda website.
   b. Download the appropriate installer for your operating system.
2. **Install Anaconda**:
   a. Run the installer and follow the instructions.
3. **Verify Installation**: Once installed, open a terminal or Anaconda prompt and type:

```
bconda list numpy
```

This will show you if NumPy is already installed in the Anaconda environment.

Chapter 2: Array Arithmetic in NumPy

This chapter delves into array arithmetic in **NumPy**, a fundamental feature that allows element-wise operations, broadcasting, and matrix operations. These capabilities enable efficient and concise computations, essential for tasks in data analysis, machine learning, and numerical simulations.

Key Characteristics of Array Arithmetic

1. **Element-Wise Operations**: Perform arithmetic operations between arrays element by element.
2. **Broadcasting**: Handles operations between arrays of different shapes by aligning dimensions where possible.
3. **Efficient Computation**: Leverages low-level optimizations for faster operations compared to native Python.
4. **Versatile Operations**: Supports scalar, vector, and matrix computations.
5. **Integration**: Works seamlessly with other NumPy functions and libraries.

Basic Rules for Array Arithmetic

1. Arrays must have compatible shapes for operations. If not, broadcasting rules are applied.
2. Arithmetic operations can be performed with scalars or other arrays.
3. Results are typically stored in a new array unless explicitly overwritten.
4. Operations follow standard mathematical rules, ensuring intuitive usage.

Best Practices

1. **Understand Broadcasting**: Ensure shapes are compatible to avoid unexpected results.
2. **Use Vectorized Operations**: Replace explicit loops with NumPy operations for better performance.

3. **Validate Data Types**: Check the dtype of arrays to avoid issues with precision or type conversion.
4. **Optimize Memory Usage**: Use in-place operations (out parameter) where applicable.
5. **Explore Ufuncs**: Utilize universal functions for additional functionality.

Syntax Table

SL No	Function/Feature	Syntax/Example	Description
1	Addition	arr1 + arr2	Adds two arrays element-wise
2	Subtraction	arr1 - arr2	Subtracts the second array from the first
3	Multiplication	arr1 * arr2	Multiplies two arrays element-wise
4	Division	arr1 / arr2	Divides the first array by the second
5	Matrix Multiplication	arr1 @ arr2 or np.dot(arr1, arr2)	Performs matrix multiplication

Syntax Explanation

1. Addition

What is Addition?

Adds corresponding elements of two arrays. If the arrays have different shapes, broadcasting rules are applied.

Syntax

arr1 + arr2

Syntax Explanation

- Arrays must be of the same shape or broadcastable.
- The result is a new array containing the sum of corresponding elements.
- Can be used for scalar addition as well.

Example

```
import numpy as np
arr1 = np.array([1, 2, 3])
arr2 = np.array([4, 5, 6])
result = arr1 + arr2
print(result)
```
Example Explanation
- Adds [1, 2, 3] to [4, 5, 6] element-wise.
- Outputs [5, 7, 9].

2. Subtraction

What is Subtraction?
Subtracts corresponding elements of one array from another.
Syntax
```
arr1 - arr2
```
Syntax Explanation
- Arrays must be of the same shape or broadcastable.
- The result is a new array containing the difference of corresponding elements.

Example
```
arr1 = np.array([10, 20, 30])
arr2 = np.array([1, 2, 3])
result = arr1 - arr2
print(result)
```
Example Explanation
- Subtracts [1, 2, 3] from [10, 20, 30] element-wise.
- Outputs [9, 18, 27].

3. Multiplication

What is Multiplication?
Multiplies corresponding elements of two arrays element-wise.
Syntax
```
arr1 * arr2
```
Syntax Explanation
- Arrays must be of the same shape or broadcastable.
- Scalar multiplication is also supported.

Example

```
arr1 = np.array([1, 2, 3])
arr2 = np.array([4, 5, 6])
result = arr1 * arr2
print(result)
```

Example Explanation

- Multiplies [1, 2, 3] with [4, 5, 6] element-wise.
- Outputs [4, 10, 18].

4. Division

What is Division?

Divides corresponding elements of one array by another element-wise.

Syntax

```
arr1 / arr2
```

Syntax Explanation

- Arrays must be of the same shape or broadcastable.
- Scalar division is also supported.

Example

```
arr1 = np.array([10, 20, 30])
arr2 = np.array([2, 4, 6])
result = arr1 / arr2
print(result)
```

Example Explanation

- Divides [10, 20, 30] by [2, 4, 6] element-wise.
- Outputs [5.0, 5.0, 5.0].

5. Matrix Multiplication

What is Matrix Multiplication?
Performs matrix multiplication between two arrays.

Syntax
```
arr1 @ arr2
# or
np.dot(arr1, arr2)
```

Syntax Explanation
- Requires arrays to have compatible shapes (e.g., (m, n) and (n, p)).
- Produces a new array of shape (m, p).
- Does not perform element-wise multiplication.

Example
```
arr1 = np.array([[1, 2], [3, 4]])
arr2 = np.array([[5, 6], [7, 8]])
result = arr1 @ arr2
print(result)
```

Example Explanation
- Multiplies matrices [[1, 2], [3, 4]] and [[5, 6], [7, 8]].
- Outputs [[19, 22], [43, 50]].

Real-Life Project

Project Name: Linear Regression Computation
Project Goal Implement the core computations of linear regression using NumPy's array arithmetic capabilities.

Code for This Project

```python
import numpy as np

def linear_regression(X, y):
    # Adding bias term to X
    X = np.hstack((np.ones((X.shape[0], 1)), X))
    # Computing weights using the Normal Equation
    weights = np.linalg.inv(X.T @ X) @ X.T @ y
    return weights

# Example usage
X = np.array([[1], [2], [3]])  # Feature matrix
y = np.array([2, 4, 6])        # Target values
weights = linear_regression(X, y)
print("Weights:", weights)
```

Expanded Features
- Adds a bias term for intercept calculation.
- Utilizes matrix multiplication for efficient computation.
- Demonstrates use of NumPy's `np.linalg.inv` and `@` operator.

Expected Output
```
Weights: [0. 2.]
```

This output demonstrates the computation of weights in a simple linear regression model, highlighting the relationship between features and target values.

Chapter 3: Mathematical Functions in NumPy

This chapter explores the extensive mathematical functions available in NumPy, enabling complex computations with minimal effort. NumPy provides a wide range of mathematical operations, including trigonometric, exponential, logarithmic, and statistical functions. These functions are essential for scientific computing, data processing, and numerical simulations.

Key Characteristics of Mathematical Functions in NumPy:

- **Comprehensive Library:** Offers a wide variety of functions for mathematical operations.
- **High Performance:** Optimized for speed and efficiency, leveraging vectorized operations.
- **Support for Arrays:** Functions are designed to work seamlessly with NumPy arrays of any shape.
- **Broadcasting Compatibility:** Handles operations on arrays with different shapes via broadcasting.
- **Consistency:** Ensures precise and predictable behavior across different platforms.

Basic Rules for Mathematical Functions:

- Functions operate element-wise on arrays unless otherwise specified.
- Support for scalars and arrays, making them flexible for different use cases.
- Compatible with both integer and floating-point data types.
- Return new arrays as outputs, leaving original inputs unaltered unless explicitly specified.
- Handle special cases like infinity and NaN gracefully.

Best Practices:

- **Use Vectorized Functions:** Replace explicit loops with NumPy's built-in functions for better performance.
- **Combine Functions:** Chain multiple operations for concise and efficient code.
- **Validate Input Types:** Ensure input arrays have appropriate data

types to avoid errors or precision loss.

- **Handle Edge Cases:** Check for special cases like division by zero or logarithm of non-positive values.
- **Leverage Documentation:** Refer to official documentation for a complete list of available functions and their use cases.

Syntax Table:

SL No	Function/Feature	Syntax/Example	Description
1	Sine	np.sin(arr)	Computes the sine of each element.
2	Exponential	np.exp(arr)	Computes the exponential (e^x) of elements.
3	Logarithm	np.log(arr)	Computes the natural logarithm.
4	Square Root	np.sqrt(arr)	Computes the square root of elements.
5	Absolute Value	np.abs(arr)	Computes the absolute value of elements.

Syntax Explanation:

1. Sine

What is Sine?
Calculates the sine of each element in the array. Input values should be in radians.

Syntax:
np.sin(arr)

Syntax Explanation:
- Operates element-wise on arrays.
- Supports both scalars and arrays.
- Returns a new array containing the sine values of input elements.

Example:
```
import numpy as np
arr = np.array([0, np.pi/2, np.pi])
result = np.sin(arr)
```

```
print(result)
```

Example Explanation:
- Computes the sine of [0, π/2, π].
- Outputs [0.0, 1.0, 0.0].

2. Exponential

What is Exponential?
Calculates the exponential (e^x) of each element in the array.
Syntax:
```
np.exp(arr)
```

Syntax Explanation:
- Operates element-wise on arrays.
- Supports both scalars and arrays.
- Returns a new array with exponential values of input elements.

Example:
```
arr = np.array([0, 1, 2])
result = np.exp(arr)
print(result)
```

Example Explanation:
- Computes the exponential of [0, 1, 2].
- Outputs [1.0, 2.71828183, 7.3890561].

3. Logarithm

What is Logarithm?
Calculates the natural logarithm (log base e) of each element in the array.
Syntax:
```
np.log(arr)
```
Syntax Explanation:
- Input array elements must be positive.
- Operates element-wise and returns a new array.

Example:
```
arr = np.array([1, np.e, np.e**2])
result = np.log(arr)
```

```
print(result)
```
Example Explanation:
- Computes the logarithm of [1, e, e^2].
- Outputs [0.0, 1.0, 2.0].

4. Square Root

What is Square Root?
Calculates the square root of each element in the array.
Syntax:
```
np.sqrt(arr)
```
Syntax Explanation:
- Input elements must be non-negative.
- Operates element-wise and returns a new array.

Example:
```
arr = np.array([4, 9, 16])
result = np.sqrt(arr)
print(result)
```
Example Explanation:
- Computes the square root of [4, 9, 16].
- Outputs [2.0, 3.0, 4.0].

5. Absolute Value

What is Absolute Value?
Calculates the absolute value of each element in the array.
Syntax:
```
np.abs(arr)
```
Syntax Explanation:
- Operates element-wise.
- Works with integers, floats, and complex numbers.

Example:
```
arr = np.array([-1, -2, 3])
result = np.abs(arr)
print(result)
```
Example Explanation:
- Computes the absolute value of [-1, -2, 3].

- Outputs [1, 2, 3].

Real-Life Project

Project Name: Data Normalization
Project Goal:
Normalize a dataset to bring all values within a specific range using NumPy's mathematical functions.

Code for This Project:

```python
import numpy as np

def normalize(data):
    # Compute the mean and standard deviation
    mean = np.mean(data)
    std = np.std(data)
    # Normalize the data
    normalized_data = (data - mean) / std
    return normalized_data

# Example usage
data = np.array([10, 20, 30, 40, 50])
normalized_data = normalize(data)
print("Normalized Data:", normalized_data)
```

Expanded Features:

- Uses np.mean and np.std for statistical computation.
- Demonstrates chaining of array arithmetic with mathematical functions.
- Highlights the use of mathematical functions in real-world data processing tasks.

Expected Output:
Normalized Data: [-1.41421356, -0.70710678, 0.0, 0.70710678, 1.41421356]
This output demonstrates the normalization process, bringing all values into a standard scale for further analysis or machine learning applications.

Chapter 4: Aggregations in NumPy

This chapter focuses on aggregation functions in NumPy, which are used to summarize data. Aggregations include computing sums, means, medians, variances, and more. These functions are essential for statistical analysis, data preprocessing, and scientific research.

Key Characteristics of Aggregations in NumPy:

- **Efficiency:** Optimized for large datasets, making operations fast and memory-efficient.
- **Wide Variety:** Includes common statistical functions such as mean, median, standard deviation, and sum.
- **Axis Support:** Allows aggregation over specific axes for multidimensional arrays.
- **Element-Wise Operations:** Functions operate efficiently across all elements of an array.
- **Integration:** Seamlessly integrates with other NumPy functionalities for comprehensive data analysis.

Basic Rules for Aggregations:

- Aggregation functions operate element-wise by default, summarizing the entire array.
- For multidimensional arrays, the `axis` parameter specifies which axis to aggregate.
- Functions return a scalar or a reduced array based on the input dimensions.
- Missing data (e.g., NaN) can be handled using specialized functions such as `np.nanmean` or `np.nansum`.

Best Practices:

- **Use Axis Parameter:** Specify the axis for multidimensional data to control the aggregation scope.
- **Handle Missing Data:** Use nan-safe functions when working with incomplete datasets.
- **Leverage Documentation:** Explore the full range of aggregation functions for various use cases.
- **Optimize Code:** Combine aggregations with slicing or boolean indexing for efficient data manipulation.

- **Validate Data Types:** Ensure data types are compatible with the aggregation function to avoid precision loss.

Syntax Table:

SL No	Function/Feature	Syntax/Example	Description
1	Sum	np.sum(arr)	Computes the sum of all elements.
2	Mean	np.mean(arr)	Computes the average value of elements.
3	Median	np.median(arr)	Finds the median value of elements.
4	Standard Deviation	np.std(arr)	Computes the standard deviation.
5	Variance	np.var(arr)	Computes the variance of elements.

Syntax Explanation:

1. Sum

What is Sum?
Calculates the total sum of all elements in the array. It can also compute sums along specific axes.

Syntax:
np.sum(arr, axis=None)

Syntax Explanation:
- Operates element-wise across the array.
- Use the axis parameter for axis-specific aggregation.
- Returns a scalar or a reduced array based on the input.

Example:
```
import numpy as np
arr = np.array([[1, 2, 3], [4, 5, 6]])
total_sum = np.sum(arr)
row_sum = np.sum(arr, axis=1)
print("Total Sum:", total_sum)
print("Row-Wise Sum:", row_sum)
```

Example Explanation:
- Computes the total sum of all elements: 21.
- Computes the row-wise sum: [6, 15].

2. Mean

What is Mean?
Calculates the average value of all elements in the array.
Syntax:
```
np.mean(arr, axis=None)
```
Syntax Explanation:
- Operates element-wise across the array.
- Use the axis parameter for axis-specific aggregation.
- Returns a scalar or a reduced array based on the input.

Example:
```
arr = np.array([[1, 2, 3], [4, 5, 6]])
overall_mean = np.mean(arr)
column_mean = np.mean(arr, axis=0)
print("Overall Mean:", overall_mean)
print("Column-Wise Mean:", column_mean)
```
Example Explanation:
- Computes the overall mean: 3.5.
- Computes the column-wise mean: [2.5, 3.5, 4.5].

3. Median

What is Median?
Finds the median value, the middle element in a sorted sequence, of all elements in the array.
Syntax:
```
np.median(arr, axis=None)
```
Syntax Explanation:
- Operates element-wise across the array.
- Use the axis parameter for axis-specific aggregation.
- Returns a scalar or a reduced array based on the input.

Example:
```python
arr = np.array([1, 3, 5, 7, 9])
median_value = np.median(arr)
print("Median:", median_value)
```

Example Explanation:
- Computes the median of [1, 3, 5, 7, 9]: 5.

4. Standard Deviation

What is Standard Deviation?
Calculates the spread of data elements from the mean.
Syntax:
```python
np.std(arr, axis=None)
```
Syntax Explanation:
- Operates element-wise across the array.
- Use the axis parameter for axis-specific aggregation.
- Returns a scalar or a reduced array based on the input.

Example:
```python
arr = np.array([1, 2, 3, 4, 5])
std_dev = np.std(arr)
print("Standard Deviation:", std_dev)
```
Example Explanation:
- Computes the standard deviation of [1, 2, 3, 4, 5]: 1.414.

5. Variance

What is Variance?

Measures the average squared deviation of each data point from the mean.
Syntax:
```python
np.var(arr, axis=None)
```
Syntax Explanation:
- Operates element-wise across the array.
- Use the axis parameter for axis-specific aggregation.
- Returns a scalar or a reduced array based on the input.

Example:

```
arr = np.array([1, 2, 3, 4, 5])
variance = np.var(arr)
print("Variance:", variance)
```

Example Explanation:

- Computes the variance of [1, 2, 3, 4, 5]: 2.0.

Real-Life Project:

Project Name: Data Analysis Summary

Project Goal:

Summarize a dataset by calculating key aggregations such as total, mean, and variance for each feature.

Code for This Project:

```
import numpy as np
def summarize_data(data):
    total = np.sum(data, axis=0)
    mean = np.mean(data, axis=0)
    variance = np.var(data, axis=0)
    return total, mean, variance
# Example usage
data = np.array([[10, 20, 30], [40, 50, 60], [70, 80, 90]])
total, mean, variance = summarize_data(data)
print("Total:", total)
print("Mean:", mean)
print("Variance:", variance)
```

Expanded Features:

- Demonstrates aggregation across columns (features) of a dataset.
- Combines multiple aggregation functions for comprehensive analysis.
- Highlights the importance of statistical summaries in data preprocessing.

Expected Output:

```
Total: [120, 150, 180]
Mean: [40.0, 50.0, 60.0]
Variance: [800.0, 800.0, 800.0]
```

Chapter 5: Boolean and Logical Operations in NumPy

This chapter focuses on Boolean and logical operations in NumPy, which are critical for filtering data, conditionally modifying arrays, and implementing logical expressions. These operations form the foundation for data manipulation and preprocessing in scientific computing and data analysis.

Key Characteristics of Boolean and Logical Operations in NumPy:

- **Element-Wise Operations:** Logical operations are performed on each element of the array.
- **Boolean Indexing:** Use Boolean arrays to filter or modify specific elements.
- **Logical Functions:** Provides a variety of logical functions like np.logical_and, np.logical_or, and np.logical_not.
- **Support for Broadcasting:** Logical operations are compatible with broadcasting rules.
- **Integration:** Can be combined with other NumPy features like aggregations and mathematical functions.

Basic Rules for Boolean and Logical Operations:

- Comparisons generate Boolean arrays with True or False values.
- Logical operations can be combined with arithmetic or other array operations.
- Boolean arrays can be used as indices to access or modify elements in another array.
- Logical functions accept arrays or scalars as inputs and return an array of Boolean values.

Best Practices:

- **Use Boolean Indexing:** Simplify filtering and conditional operations using Boolean arrays.
- **Combine Logical Functions:** Use np.logical_and, np.logical_or, etc., for complex logical expressions.
- **Validate Input Shapes:** Ensure inputs to logical functions have compatible shapes for broadcasting.
- **Handle Missing Data:** Use np.isnan and np.isfinite to

manage missing or infinite values.

- **Optimize Conditions:** Combine conditions to minimize computational overhead.

Syntax Table:

SL No	Function/Feature	Syntax/Example	Description
1	Comparison Operators	`arr > 5`	Performs element-wise comparison.
2	Logical AND	`np.logical_and (arr1, arr2)`	Performs element-wise logical AND.
3	Logical OR	`np.logical_or( arr1, arr2)`	Performs element-wise logical OR.
4	Logical NOT	`np.logical_not (arr)`	Performs element-wise logical NOT.
5	Boolean Indexing	`arr[arr > 5]`	Filters elements based on a condition.

Syntax Explanation:

1. Comparison Operators

What are Comparison Operators?
Generate Boolean arrays by comparing elements of an array to a value or another array.
Syntax:
```
arr > value
arr1 == arr2
```
Syntax Explanation:
- Operates element-wise to compare array elements with a scalar or another array.
- Returns a Boolean array with `True` or `False` values.
- Compatible with broadcasting for arrays of different shapes.

Example:
```
import numpy as np
arr = np.array([1, 2, 3, 4, 5])
result = arr > 3
print("Comparison Result:", result)
```
Example Explanation:
- Compares each element of [1, 2, 3, 4, 5] to 3.
- Outputs [False, False, False, True, True].

2. Logical AND

What is Logical AND?

Performs an element-wise logical AND operation between two arrays.
Syntax:
```
np.logical_and(arr1, arr2)
```
Syntax Explanation:
- Operates element-wise between two arrays.
- Returns a Boolean array where each element is the logical AND of the corresponding elements in the input arrays.
- Input arrays must have the same shape or be broadcastable.

Example:
```
arr1 = np.array([True, False, True])
arr2 = np.array([False, False, True])
result = np.logical_and(arr1, arr2)
print("Logical AND Result:", result)
```
Example Explanation:
- Computes element-wise AND: [True AND False, False AND False, True AND True].
- Outputs [False, False, True].

3. Logical OR

What is Logical OR?
Performs an element-wise logical OR operation between two arrays.

Syntax:
```
np.logical_or(arr1, arr2)
```

Syntax Explanation:
- Operates element-wise between two arrays.
- Returns a Boolean array where each element is the logical OR of the corresponding elements in the input arrays.
- Input arrays must have the same shape or be broadcastable.

Example:
```
arr1 = np.array([True, False, True])
arr2 = np.array([False, False, True])
result = np.logical_or(arr1, arr2)
print("Logical OR Result:", result)
```

Example Explanation:
- Computes element-wise OR: [True OR False, False OR False, True OR True].
- Outputs [True, False, True].

4. Logical NOT

What is Logical NOT?
Performs an element-wise logical NOT operation on an array.

Syntax:
```
np.logical_not(arr)
```

Syntax Explanation:
- Operates element-wise on a single array.
- Returns a Boolean array where each element is the logical NOT of the corresponding element in the input array.

Example:
```
arr = np.array([True, False, True])
result = np.logical_not(arr)
print("Logical NOT Result:", result)
```

Example Explanation:
- Computes NOT: [NOT True, NOT False, NOT True].
- Outputs [False, True, False].

5. Boolean Indexing

What is Boolean Indexing?
Filters elements of an array based on a Boolean condition.
Syntax:
`arr[condition]`
Syntax Explanation:
- Evaluates the condition to create a Boolean array.
- Uses the Boolean array to index and filter elements in the original array.
- Returns a new array containing only the elements that satisfy the condition.

Example:
```
arr = np.array([1, 2, 3, 4, 5])
filtered = arr[arr > 3]
print("Filtered Array:", filtered)
```
Example Explanation:
- Filters elements greater than 3.
- Outputs [4, 5].

Real-Life Project:

Project Name: Conditional Data Filtering
Project Goal:
Filter and modify a dataset based on specific conditions using Boolean and logical operations.

Code for This Project:

```
import numpy as np

def filter_and_modify(data):
    # Filter elements greater than a threshold
    filtered_data = data[data > 50]
    # Modify elements based on a condition
    data[data < 50] = 0
    return filtered_data, data
```

```
# Example usage
data = np.array([10, 20, 50, 70, 90])
filtered, modified = filter_and_modify(data)
print("Filtered Data:", filtered)
print("Modified Data:", modified)
```

Expanded Features:

- Demonstrates conditional filtering and in-place modification of arrays.
- Highlights the combination of logical operations and Boolean indexing.
- Useful for preprocessing datasets in machine learning and analysis.

Expected Output:

Filtered Data: [70, 90]

Modified Data: [0, 0, 0, 70, 90]

This output illustrates how Boolean and logical operations enable efficient data manipulation and preprocessing.

Chapter 6: Sorting and Searching in NumPy

This chapter explores sorting and searching operations in NumPy, enabling efficient organization and retrieval of data. Sorting arranges elements in a specific order, while searching helps locate elements or indices based on conditions. These operations are vital for data preprocessing, analysis, and optimization tasks.

Key Characteristics of Sorting and Searching in NumPy:

- **Efficiency:** Optimized for fast sorting and searching operations.
- **Customizability:** Supports sorting based on specific axes and orders.
- **Versatility:** Provides functions for both exact matches and condition-based searches.
- **Integration:** Combines seamlessly with other NumPy functionalities.
- **Scalability:** Handles operations efficiently, even for large datasets.

Basic Rules for Sorting and Searching:

- Sorting functions reorder elements in ascending order by default.
- Searching functions return indices of matching elements or conditions.
- Operations can be performed along specific axes for multidimensional arrays.
- Inputs should have appropriate data types to ensure correct results.

Best Practices:

- **Use Axis Parameter:** Specify the axis for sorting/searching in multidimensional arrays.
- **Leverage Argsort:** Use np.argsort to retrieve sorted indices for further operations.
- **Combine Searches:** Use logical operations for compound search conditions.
- **Optimize Iterative Searches:** Use broadcasting or vectorized functions instead of loops.
- **Validate Input Data:** Ensure inputs are well-structured and free of

inconsistencies.

Syntax Table:

SL No	Function/ Feature	Syntax/Example	Description
1	Sort Array	`np.sort(arr)`	Returns a sorted copy of the array.
2	Argsort	`np.argsort(ar r)`	Returns indices that would sort the array.
3	Searchsor ted	`np.searchsort ed(arr, value)`	Finds indices where elements should be inserted.
4	Where	`np.where(cond ition)`	Returns indices of elements matching a condition.
5	Nonzero	`np.nonzero(ar r)`	Returns indices of non-zero elements.

Syntax Explanation:

1. Sort Array

What is Sort Array?

Reorders elements of an array in ascending order. For multidimensional arrays, sorting can be performed along specific axes.

Syntax:

```
np.sort(arr, axis=-1)
```

Syntax Explanation:

- Operates element-wise to sort the array.
- By default, sorts along the last axis (`axis=-1`).
- Accepts additional parameters like `kind` to specify the sorting algorithm (`quicksort`, `mergesort`, etc.).
- Returns a new sorted array without modifying the original.
- Can handle both 1D and multidimensional arrays effectively.

Example:

```
import numpy as np
arr = np.array([[3, 1, 4], [1, 5, 9]])
sorted_arr = np.sort(arr, axis=1)
print("Sorted Array:", sorted_arr)
```

Example Explanation:

- Sorts each row of the 2D array `[[3, 1, 4], [1, 5, 9]]` along the last axis.
- Outputs `[[1, 3, 4], [1, 5, 9]]`.

2. Argsort

What is Argsort?
Returns indices that would sort the array. Useful for indirect sorting or ranking.

Syntax:
```
np.argsort(arr, axis=-1)
```
Syntax Explanation:

- Operates element-wise to determine the order of indices for sorting.
- By default, sorts along the last axis (`axis=-1`).
- Returns an array of indices representing the order.
- Can be used for sorting related data using the indices.

Example:
```
arr = np.array([50, 20, 80, 40, 60])
sorted_indices = np.argsort(arr)
print("Sorted Indices:", sorted_indices)
```
Example Explanation:

- Determines the indices that sort `[50, 20, 80, 40, 60]`.
- Outputs `[1, 3, 0, 4, 2]`.
- Using these indices, you can sort other related arrays in the same order.

3. Searchsorted

What is Searchsorted?
Finds indices where elements should be inserted to maintain order.

Syntax:
```
np.searchsorted(arr, value, side='left')
```
Syntax Explanation:

- Assumes the input array is sorted in ascending order.

- value: The value(s) to locate in the array.
- side: Specifies insertion point preference:
    - 'left': Finds the first suitable index.
    - 'right': Finds the last suitable index.
- Handles multiple values for insertion by accepting an array of value.

Example:
```
arr = np.array([10, 20, 30, 40])
index = np.searchsorted(arr, [25, 35])
print("Insertion Indices:", index)
```
Example Explanation:
- Determines where 25 and 35 should be inserted to maintain order.
- Outputs [2, 3].

4. Where

What is Where?

Returns indices of elements matching a condition.
Syntax:
```
np.where(condition)
```
Syntax Explanation:
- Evaluates the condition element-wise.
- Returns a tuple of arrays containing indices for each dimension where the condition is True.
- Can also be used to perform conditional assignments when combined with optional parameters.

Example:
```
arr = np.array([10, 20, 30, 40, 50])
indices = np.where(arr > 25)
print("Indices:", indices)
```
Example Explanation:
- Finds indices where elements of [10, 20, 30, 40, 50] are greater than 25.
- Outputs (array([2, 3, 4]),).

5. Nonzero

What is Nonzero?
Returns indices of non-zero elements in the array.
Syntax:
```
np.nonzero(arr)
```
Syntax Explanation:
- Evaluates the array element-wise.
- Returns a tuple of arrays where each element corresponds to the indices of a non-zero element in the original array.
- Useful for filtering or indexing operations where non-zero values are significant.

Example:
```
arr = np.array([[0, 1, 0], [2, 0, 3]])
indices = np.nonzero(arr)
print("Nonzero Indices:", indices)
```
Example Explanation:
- Finds indices of non-zero elements in [[0, 1, 0], [2, 0, 3]].
- Outputs (array([0, 1, 1]), array([1, 0, 2])).
- The result indicates the row and column indices of non-zero elements.

Real-Life Project:

Project Name: Rank and Filter Dataset
Project Goal:
Sort, rank, and filter a dataset based on specific conditions.
Code for This Project:
```
import numpy as np
def rank_and_filter(data, threshold):
    # Rank elements using argsort
    ranks = np.argsort(data)
    # Filter elements above the threshold
    filtered = data[data > threshold]
    return ranks, filtered
```

```
# Example usage
data = np.array([50, 20, 80, 40, 60])
ranks, filtered = rank_and_filter(data, 50)
print("Ranks:", ranks)
print("Filtered Data:", filtered)
```

Expanded Features:

- Demonstrates combined use of sorting and filtering operations.
- Highlights practical applications like ranking and thresholding datasets.
- Useful for preprocessing and analysis in machine learning and data science.

Expected Output:

Ranks: [1, 3, 0, 4, 2]

Filtered Data: [80, 60]

This output showcases the power of sorting and searching operations in organizing and filtering data efficiently.

Chapter 7: Reshaping Arrays with NumPy

This chapter explores reshaping operations in NumPy, which are essential for organizing and structuring data effectively. Reshaping transforms arrays into different shapes without altering their data, making it a fundamental tool in data analysis and preprocessing.

Key Characteristics of Reshaping in NumPy:

- **Flexibility:** Convert arrays into any shape compatible with the total number of elements.
- **Data Integrity:** Reshaping does not alter the original data values.
- **Compatibility:** Integrates seamlessly with other NumPy operations.
- **Efficiency:** Performs operations with minimal computational overhead.
- **Multi-Dimensional Support:** Handles both 1D and multi-dimensional arrays.

Basic Rules for Reshaping:

- The total number of elements must remain constant.
- Reshaping operations return a new view of the array when possible, sharing data with the original.
- Use -1 as a placeholder for dimensions to let NumPy infer the appropriate size.

Best Practices:

- **Check Array Shape:** Use `arr.shape` to understand the current dimensions before reshaping.
- **Validate Dimensions:** Ensure the target shape is compatible with the total elements.
- **Leverage Views:** Modify reshaped arrays carefully as they may share data with the original.
- **Use Flattening Sparingly:** Avoid unnecessary flattening and re-reshaping operations to maintain efficiency.
- **Explore Utilities:** Use utility functions like `np.ravel` or `np.flatten` for specific use cases.

Syntax Table:

SL No	Function/Feature	Syntax/Example	Description
1	Reshape	`np.reshape(arr, newshape)`	Changes the shape of an array.
2	Ravel	`np.ravel(arr)`	Flattens the array into a 1D view.
3	Transpose	`np.transpose(arr)`	Reverses or permutes array axes.
4	Expand Dimensions	`np.expand_dims(arr, axis)`	Adds a new axis to the array.
5	Squeeze	`np.squeeze(arr, axis=None)`	Removes axes of size 1.

Syntax Explanation:

1. Reshape

What is Reshape?
Reshapes an array to a specified shape without changing its data.
Syntax:
`np.reshape(arr, newshape)`
Syntax Explanation:
- arr: The input array to reshape.
- newshape: A tuple specifying the desired dimensions of the reshaped array.
  - One of the dimensions can be -1, which allows NumPy to automatically calculate its size based on the total number of elements.
- Returns a reshaped view of the original array if possible; otherwise, a new array is created.
- The product of the dimensions in newshape must equal the total number of elements in the original array.
- The reshaped array shares data with the original array, meaning modifications to one may affect the other.

Example:
```
import numpy as np
arr = np.array([1, 2, 3, 4, 5, 6])
reshaped = np.reshape(arr, (2, 3))
print("Reshaped Array:", reshaped)
```
Example Explanation:
- Converts a 1D array [1, 2, 3, 4, 5, 6] into a 2x3 array.
- Outputs [[1, 2, 3], [4, 5, 6]].
- If the specified dimensions do not match the total number of elements, NumPy raises a ValueError.

2. Ravel

What is Ravel?
Flattens an array into a contiguous 1D view.
Syntax:
```
np.ravel(arr)
```

Syntax Explanation:
- arr: The input array to be flattened.
- Returns a flattened 1D view of the original array.
- Modifying the returned array may also modify the original array if they share memory.
- Unlike np.flatten, np.ravel always attempts to return a view rather than a copy for better performance.

Example:
```
arr = np.array([[1, 2], [3, 4]])
flattened = np.ravel(arr)
print("Flattened Array:", flattened)
```
Example Explanation:
- Flattens [[1, 2], [3, 4]] into [1, 2, 3, 4].
- This operation is memory-efficient because it returns a view when possible.

3. Transpose

What is Transpose?
Reverses or permutes the axes of an array.
Syntax:
```
np.transpose(arr, axes=None)
```
Syntax Explanation:
- arr: The input array to transpose.
- axes: Optional sequence specifying the order of axes in the result. If not provided, reverses the order of axes by default.
- Returns a view with the axes permuted.
- Useful for switching rows and columns in 2D arrays or rearranging dimensions in higher-dimensional arrays.

Example:
```
arr = np.array([[1, 2, 3], [4, 5, 6]])
transposed = np.transpose(arr)
print("Transposed Array:", transposed)
```
Example Explanation:
- Transposes the 2D array [[1, 2, 3], [4, 5, 6]] by swapping rows and columns.
- Outputs [[1, 4], [2, 5], [3, 6]].

4. Expand Dimensions

What is Expand Dimensions?
Adds a new axis to the array at the specified position.
Syntax:
```
np.expand_dims(arr, axis)
```

Syntax Explanation:
- arr: The input array to expand.
- axis: Position where the new axis should be added. Negative values count from the last axis.
- Returns a view of the array with an additional dimension.
- Useful for aligning shapes of arrays for broadcasting or computations.

Example:
```
arr = np.array([1, 2, 3])
expanded = np.expand_dims(arr, axis=0)
print("Expanded Array:", expanded)
```

Example Explanation:
- Expands the shape of [1, 2, 3] from (3,) to (1, 3) by adding a new axis at position 0.

5. Squeeze

What is Squeeze?
Removes axes of size 1 from the array.
Syntax:
```
np.squeeze(arr, axis=None)
```

Syntax Explanation:
- arr: The input array to squeeze.
- axis: Optional; specifies which axes to squeeze. If not provided, all axes of size 1 are removed.
- Returns a view with reduced dimensions, removing single-dimensional entries.
- Raises a ValueError if a specified axis is not of size 1.

Example:
```
arr = np.array([[[1], [2], [3]]])
squeezed = np.squeeze(arr)
print("Squeezed Array:", squeezed)
```

Example Explanation:
- Removes axes of size 1 from the array [[[1], [2], [3]]].
- Outputs [1, 2, 3].

Real-Life Project:

Project Name: Reshape and Process Data
Project Goal:
Reshape and preprocess a dataset for analysis or machine learning.
Code for This Project:
```python
import numpy as np
def preprocess_data(data):
    # Reshape to 2D
    reshaped = np.reshape(data, (-1, 4))
    # Transpose for easier analysis
    transposed = np.transpose(reshaped)
    return reshaped, transposed
# Example usage
data = np.arange(16)
reshaped, transposed = preprocess_data(data)
print("Reshaped Data:\n", reshaped)
print("Transposed Data:\n", transposed)
```
Expanded Features:
- Demonstrates combining reshaping and transposing for preprocessing.
- Highlights practical use in reorganizing datasets.
- Useful for tasks like feature engineering in machine learning.

Expected Output:
Reshaped Data:
```
[[ 0  1  2  3]
 [ 4  5  6  7]
 [ 8  9 10 11]
 [12 13 14 15]]
```
Transposed Data:
```
[[ 0  4  8 12]
 [ 1  5  9 13]
 [ 2  6 10 14]
 [ 3  7 11 15]]
```

This project illustrates the power of reshaping operations in preparing data for various analytical workflows.

Chapter 8: Broadcasting in Depth with NumPy

Broadcasting in NumPy is a powerful mechanism that allows operations on arrays of different shapes. It simplifies coding and enhances performance by eliminating the need for explicit loops. Understanding broadcasting is essential for efficient data manipulation and computation.

Key Characteristics of Broadcasting:

- **Dimension Alignment:** Extends smaller arrays to match the shape of larger arrays without creating copies.
- **Memory Efficiency:** Performs operations without duplicating data, saving memory.
- **Automation:** Handles shape mismatches seamlessly when rules are satisfied.
- **Flexibility:** Works with scalars and arrays of different dimensions.
- **Integration:** Supports element-wise operations and other NumPy functions.

Basic Rules for Broadcasting:

1. Dimensions of arrays are compared from right to left.
2. Arrays are compatible when:
    a. They have the same shape, or
    b. One of the dimensions is 1.
3. Missing dimensions are implicitly added to the left of the smaller array.
4. If the rules are not satisfied, NumPy raises a `ValueError`.

Best Practices:

- **Validate Shapes:** Check shapes with `arr.shape` to ensure compatibility before operations.
- **Leverage Broadcasting:** Avoid manually expanding arrays; rely on NumPy for efficiency.
- **Understand Errors:** Use debugging tools to analyze shape mismatches.
- **Use Slicing with Broadcasting:** Simplify slicing operations to modify parts of arrays.
- **Combine Broadcasting with Aggregations:** Chain operations for

concise and efficient code.

Syntax Table:

SL No	Function/Feature	Syntax/Example	Description
1	Scalar Broadcasting	`arr + scalar`	Adds a scalar to each element of the array.
2	Array Broadcasting	`arr1 + arr2`	Performs element-wise operations on arrays.
3	Explicit Expansion	`np.expand_dims(arr, axis)`	Expands dimensions to enable broadcasting.
4	Broadcasting with Axis	`np.sum(arr, axis=...)`	Applies reductions along specified axes.
5	Outer Operations	`np.add.outer(arr1, arr2)`	Computes all pairwise operations.

Syntax Explanation:

1. Scalar Broadcasting

What is Scalar Broadcasting?
Extends scalar values to match the shape of an array for element-wise operations.
Syntax:
`arr + scalar`
Syntax Explanation:
- arr: The input array.
- scalar: The scalar value to be broadcast.
- Performs element-wise addition, applying the scalar to each element of the array.
- No explicit expansion is needed.

Example:
`import numpy as np`

```
arr = np.array([1, 2, 3])
result = arr + 5
print("Broadcasted Array:", result)
```

Example Explanation:
- Adds 5 to each element of [1, 2, 3].
- Outputs [6, 7, 8].

2. Array Broadcasting

What is Array Broadcasting?
Enables operations between arrays of different shapes by aligning their dimensions.
Syntax:
```
arr1 + arr2
```
Syntax Explanation:
- arr1 and arr2: Input arrays with compatible shapes.
- Dimensions are aligned according to broadcasting rules.
- Element-wise addition or other operations are performed.

Example:
```
arr1 = np.array([[1, 2, 3], [4, 5, 6]])
arr2 = np.array([10, 20, 30])
result = arr1 + arr2
print("Broadcasted Array:", result)
```
Example Explanation:
- Broadcasts [10, 20, 30] to match the shape of [[1, 2, 3], [4, 5, 6]].
- Outputs [[11, 22, 33], [14, 25, 36]].

3. Explicit Expansion

What is Explicit Expansion?
Manually expands dimensions of an array to enable broadcasting.
Syntax:
```
np.expand_dims(arr, axis)
```
Syntax Explanation:
- arr: The input array.

- axis: Specifies where to add the new dimension.
- Returns a view with expanded dimensions, aligning shapes for broadcasting.

Example:
```
arr = np.array([1, 2, 3])
expanded = np.expand_dims(arr, axis=0)
print("Expanded Array:", expanded)
```

Example Explanation:
- Expands [1, 2, 3] to [[1, 2, 3]], adding a new axis at position 0.
- Enables operations with arrays of shape (n, 3).

4. Broadcasting with Axis

What is Broadcasting with Axis?
Performs reductions or operations along specific axes while maintaining compatibility with other arrays.

Syntax:
```
np.sum(arr, axis=...)
```

Syntax Explanation:
- arr: The input array.
- axis: Specifies the axis or axes to reduce.
- Reduces dimensions while ensuring compatibility for broadcasting.

Example:
```
arr = np.array([[1, 2], [3, 4]])
sum_result = np.sum(arr, axis=0)
print("Summed Array:", sum_result)
```

Example Explanation:
- Sums along axis 0 (columns) for [[1, 2], [3, 4]].
- Outputs [4, 6].

5. Outer Operations

What is Outer Operations?

Computes pairwise operations between elements of two arrays, producing higher-dimensional results.

Syntax:

```
np.add.outer(arr1, arr2)
```

Syntax Explanation:

- arr1 and arr2: Input arrays.
- Computes pairwise addition for all combinations of elements.
- Outputs an array with shape (len(arr1), len(arr2)).

Example:

```
arr1 = np.array([1, 2, 3])
arr2 = np.array([10, 20])
outer_result = np.add.outer(arr1, arr2)
print("Outer Result:", outer_result)
```

Example Explanation:

- Computes all pairwise sums between [1, 2, 3] and [10, 20].
- Outputs [[11, 21], [12, 22], [13, 23]].

Real-Life Project:

Project Name: Broadcasting in Data Analysis

Project Goal:

Apply broadcasting to standardize a dataset by subtracting the mean and dividing by the standard deviation.

Code for This Project:

```
import numpy as np

def standardize_data(data):
    mean = np.mean(data, axis=0)
    std = np.std(data, axis=0)
    standardized = (data - mean) / std
    return standardized

# Example usage
data = np.array([[1, 2, 3], [4, 5, 6], [7, 8, 9]])
```

```
standardized_data = standardize_data(data)
print("Standardized Data:\n", standardized_data)
```

Expanded Features:

- Demonstrates broadcasting to align array shapes during operations.
- Highlights applications in data preprocessing and feature scaling.
- Efficiently standardizes datasets for machine learning.

Expected Output:

Standardized Data:

```
[[-1.22474487 -1.22474487 -1.22474487]
 [ 0.          0.          0.        ]
 [ 1.22474487  1.22474487  1.22474487]]
```

This output demonstrates the utility of broadcasting for efficient, large-scale data analysis.

Chapter 9: Advanced Indexing in NumPy

Advanced indexing in NumPy provides powerful tools to access, modify, and manipulate arrays with high flexibility. By leveraging integer arrays, Boolean arrays, and mixed indexing, users can perform complex data extraction and transformation operations.

Key Characteristics of Advanced Indexing:
- **Boolean Indexing:** Selects elements based on conditions, enabling filtering operations.
- **Integer Indexing:** Uses integer arrays to specify the indices for data retrieval.
- **Mixed Indexing:** Combines basic and advanced indexing methods for more granular control.
- **Broadcasting Compatibility:** Aligns indices and data dimensions seamlessly.
- **Write-Back Support:** Allows modification of original arrays using indexed subsets.

Basic Rules for Advanced Indexing:
1. Advanced indexing always returns a copy of the data, unlike basic slicing, which returns a view.
2. Index arrays must have compatible shapes for broadcasting.
3. Boolean indexing requires the Boolean array to match the shape of the array being indexed.
4. Integer indexing retrieves elements based on specified positions.

Best Practices:
- **Validate Shapes:** Ensure index arrays match the expected shapes for the desired operation.
- **Combine Indexing Methods:** Use mixed indexing for complex data extraction.
- **Optimize Boolean Masks:** Minimize redundant operations in Boolean indexing for efficiency.
- **Use np.ix_ for Multidimensional Indexing:** Create index arrays for higher-dimensional operations.
- **Avoid Overlapping Writes:** Prevent unexpected results by avoiding overlapping assignments in indexed writes.

Syntax Table:

SL No	Function/Feature	Syntax/Example	Description
1	Boolean Indexing	arr[condition]	Filters elements based on a condition.
2	Integer Indexing	arr[[i1, i2], [j1, j2]]	Retrieves elements at specified positions.
3	Mixed Indexing	arr[i, :, j]	Combines basic and advanced indexing.
4	np.ix_	np.ix_([i1, i2], [j1, j2])	Creates broadcastable index arrays.
5	Modify with Indexing	arr[indices] = value	Modifies elements at specified indices.

Syntax Explanation:

1. Boolean Indexing

What is Boolean Indexing?
Filters elements of an array using a Boolean condition.
Syntax:
arr[condition]
Syntax Explanation:
- arr: The input array from which elements are to be filtered.
- condition: A Boolean array or an expression that evaluates to a Boolean array.
  - The Boolean array must be the same shape as arr.
  - Each True value in the Boolean array corresponds to an element in arr that will be included in the output.
- Returns a new array containing only the elements where condition is True.
- Can be used with scalar comparisons, logical operations, or functions to generate the condition.

Example:
import numpy as np

```
arr = np.array([10, 20, 30, 40])
result = arr[arr > 25]
print("Filtered Elements:", result)
```

Example Explanation:
- The condition arr > 25 generates a Boolean array: [False, False, True, True].
- Elements corresponding to True values are selected: [30, 40].

2. Integer Indexing

What is Integer Indexing?
Retrieves elements at specific positions using integer arrays.
Syntax:
```
arr[[i1, i2], [j1, j2]]
```

Syntax Explanation:
- arr: The input array to index.
- [i1, i2] and [j1, j2]: Integer arrays specifying row and column indices, respectively.
  - The arrays must have the same shape.
- Returns an array where each element corresponds to the position (i, j) from the provided indices.
- Useful for non-sequential or custom indexing patterns.

Example:
```
arr = np.array([[1, 2], [3, 4]])
elements = arr[[0, 1], [1, 0]]
print("Selected Elements:", elements)
```

Example Explanation:
- Index (0,1) corresponds to 2, and (1,0) corresponds to 3.
- Outputs [2, 3].
- Allows for flexible retrieval of non-contiguous elements.

3. Mixed Indexing

What is Mixed Indexing?

Combines basic slicing and advanced indexing for complex operations.

Syntax:
```
arr[i, :, j]
```

Syntax Explanation:
- i: An integer or array specifying the slice or row index.
- : : Basic slicing to select all elements along a dimension.
- j: Integer or array specifying the column index or other dimension.
- Combines standard slicing (:) with advanced indexing (integers or arrays) to extract or manipulate specific sections of the array.

Example:
```
arr = np.array([[[1, 2], [3, 4]], [[5, 6], [7, 8]]])
result = arr[1, :, 1]
print("Mixed Indexed Elements:", result)
```

Example Explanation:
- Selects the second 2D slice ([5, 6], [7, 8]) and retrieves the second element of each row.
- Outputs [6, 8].

4. np.ix_

What is np.ix_?
Creates index arrays for broadcasting.

Syntax:
```
np.ix_([i1, i2], [j1, j2])
```

Syntax Explanation:
- np.ix_: A function to generate index arrays that can be broadcast together.
- [i1, i2]: Row indices.
- [j1, j2]: Column indices.
- Returns a tuple of arrays that allow advanced multidimensional indexing.

Example:
```
arr = np.array([[1, 2, 3], [4, 5, 6], [7, 8, 9]])
```

```
ix = np.ix_([0, 2], [1, 2])
result = arr[ix]
print("Indexed Subarray:", result)
```

Example Explanation:
- Selects rows 0 and 2 and columns 1 and 2.
- Outputs [[2, 3], [8, 9]].
- Efficiently handles multidimensional slices without manual broadcasting.

5. Modify with Indexing

What is Modify with Indexing?
Changes values at specified indices.
Syntax:
```
arr[indices] = value
```

Syntax Explanation:
- arr: The input array to modify.
- indices: Positions to update.
- value: The new value(s) to assign.
  - If value is a scalar, it is applied to all specified indices.
  - If value is an array, its shape must match the indexed subset.
- Performs in-place modifications on the original array.

Example:
```
arr = np.array([10, 20, 30, 40])
arr[arr > 25] = 0
print("Modified Array:", arr)
```
Example Explanation:
- The condition arr > 25 identifies elements 30 and 40.
- These elements are set to 0.
- Outputs [10, 20, 0, 0].

Real-Life Project:

Project Name: Extract and Transform Data

Project Goal:

Use advanced indexing to extract and manipulate data for analysis or feature engineering.

Code for This Project:

```python
import numpy as np

def process_data(data):
    # Extract rows where the first column is greater
than 50
    filtered_rows = data[data[:, 0] > 50]
    # Replace negative values in the second column with
zero
    data[data[:, 1] < 0, 1] = 0
    return filtered_rows, data

# Example usage
data = np.array([[10, -1], [60, 5], [80, -10], [90,
15]])
filtered, modified = process_data(data)
print("Filtered Rows:\n", filtered)
print("Modified Data:\n", modified)
```

Expected Output:

Filtered Rows:
```
[[60   5]
 [80 -10]
 [90  15]]
```
Modified Data:
```
[[10   0]
 [60   5]
 [80   0]
 [90  15]]
```

This project illustrates the flexibility and power of advanced indexing in transforming and analyzing data effectively.

Chapter 10: Joining and Splitting Arrays in NumPy

Joining and splitting arrays are fundamental operations in NumPy that allow you to combine and separate arrays efficiently. These operations are essential for organizing data and performing tasks like concatenation, restructuring, and splitting datasets.

Key Characteristics of Joining and Splitting:
- **Efficiency:** Operations are optimized for speed and memory usage.
- **Flexibility:** Handles arrays of different shapes when dimensions are aligned.
- **Axis Support:** Allows combining and splitting along specified axes.
- **Integration:** Works seamlessly with other NumPy functionalities.

Basic Rules for Joining and Splitting:
1. Arrays must have compatible shapes along the specified axis.
2. The `axis` parameter determines the dimension for concatenation or splitting.
3. Joining merges multiple arrays into one, while splitting divides an array into multiple subarrays.

Best Practices:
- **Validate Dimensions:** Ensure that shapes are compatible for joining or splitting.
- **Use Axis Parameter Effectively:** Leverage the `axis` parameter for precise control.
- **Optimize Performance:** Avoid excessive copying by using views where applicable.
- **Combine with Reshaping:** Reshape arrays before joining or splitting to meet requirements.
- **Handle Edge Cases:** Manage scenarios like uneven splits or empty arrays gracefully.

Syntax Table:

SL No	Function/Feature	Syntax/Example	Description
1	Concatenate Arrays	`np.concatenate((arr 1, arr2), axis=0)`	Joins arrays along an existing axis.
2	Stack Arrays	`np.stack((arr1, arr2), axis=0)`	Joins arrays along a new axis.
3	Hstack	`np.hstack((arr1, arr2))`	Joins arrays horizontally.
4	Vstack	`np.vstack((arr1, arr2))`	Joins arrays vertically.
5	Split Arrays	`np.split(arr, indices_or_sections )`	Divides an array into subarrays.
6	Hsplit	`np.hsplit(arr, indices_or_sections )`	Splits an array horizontally.
7	Vsplit	`np.vsplit(arr, indices_or_sections )`	Splits an array vertically.

Syntax Explanation:

1. Concatenate Arrays

What is Concatenate?
Combines multiple arrays into one along an existing axis.
Syntax:
`np.concatenate((arr1, arr2), axis=0)`
Syntax Explanation:
- `arr1, arr2`: Arrays to concatenate.
- `axis`: The axis along which the arrays are concatenated.
    - `axis=0` (default): Concatenates along rows.
    - `axis=1`: Concatenates along columns.
- Returns a new array combining the input arrays.
Example:

```
import numpy as np
arr1 = np.array([[1, 2], [3, 4]])
arr2 = np.array([[5, 6]])
result = np.concatenate((arr1, arr2), axis=0)
print("Concatenated Array:\n", result)
```
Example Explanation:
- Joins [[1, 2], [3, 4]] and [[5, 6]] along rows.
- Outputs: [[1, 2]
      [3, 4]
      [5, 6]]

2. Stack Arrays

What is Stack?

Combines arrays along a new axis.
Syntax:
```
np.stack((arr1, arr2), axis=0)
```

Syntax Explanation:
- arr1, arr2: Arrays to stack.
- axis: Specifies the axis for stacking.
  - Adds a new dimension to the result.
- Input arrays must have the same shape.

Example:
```
arr1 = np.array([1, 2])
arr2 = np.array([3, 4])
result = np.stack((arr1, arr2), axis=0)
print("Stacked Array:\n", result)
```

Example Explanation:
- Stacks [1, 2] and [3, 4] along a new axis.
- Outputs: [[1, 2]
      [3, 4]]

3. Hstack

What is Hstack?

Combines arrays horizontally (along columns).

Syntax:

```
np.hstack((arr1, arr2))
```

Syntax Explanation:

- `arr1`, `arr2`: Arrays to stack horizontally.
- Concatenates arrays along their second dimension (axis 1).
- Input arrays must have the same number of rows.

Example:

```
arr1 = np.array([[1], [2]])
arr2 = np.array([[3], [4]])
result = np.hstack((arr1, arr2))
print("Horizontally Stacked Array:\n", result)
```

Example Explanation:

- Joins `[[1], [2]]` and `[[3], [4]]` horizontally.
- Outputs: `[[1, 3]`
      `[2, 4]]`

4. Vstack

What is Vstack?

Combines arrays vertically (along rows).

Syntax:

```
np.vstack((arr1, arr2))
```

Syntax Explanation:

- `arr1`, `arr2`: Arrays to stack vertically.
- Concatenates arrays along their first dimension (axis 0).
- Input arrays must have the same number of columns.

Example:

```
arr1 = np.array([1, 2])
arr2 = np.array([3, 4])
result = np.vstack((arr1, arr2))
print("Vertically Stacked Array:\n", result)
```

Example Explanation:

- Stacks [1, 2] and [3, 4] vertically.
- Outputs: [[1, 2]
  [3, 4]]

5. Split Arrays

What is Split?
Divides an array into multiple subarrays along a specified axis.
Syntax:
```
np.split(arr, indices_or_sections)
```

Syntax Explanation:
- arr: The array to split.
- indices_or_sections: Specifies where to split:
  o Integer: Number of equal-sized subarrays.
  o List: Indices where the splits occur.
- Returns a list of subarrays.

Example:
```
arr = np.array([1, 2, 3, 4, 5, 6])
result = np.split(arr, 3)
print("Split Arrays:", result)
```

Example Explanation:
- Divides [1, 2, 3, 4, 5, 6] into 3 equal parts.
- Outputs: [array([1, 2]), array([3, 4]), array([5, 6])]

Real-Life Project:

Project Name: Data Merging and Partitioning
Project Goal:

Use joining and splitting operations to merge and partition datasets for preprocessing.

Code for This Project:

```python
import numpy as np

def process_datasets(data1, data2):
    # Merge datasets vertically
    merged = np.vstack((data1, data2))
    # Split merged data into training and testing
subsets
    train, test = np.split(merged, [int(0.8 *
len(merged))])
    return train, test

# Example usage
data1 = np.array([[1, 2], [3, 4]])
data2 = np.array([[5, 6], [7, 8]])
train, test = process_datasets(data1, data2)
print("Training Data:\n", train)
print("Testing Data:\n", test)
```

Expanded Features:
- Demonstrates vertical merging and splitting of datasets.
- Useful for preparing data in machine learning workflows.
- Handles operations efficiently, even with large datasets.

Expected Output:

Training Data:
```
[[1 2]
 [3 4]
 [5 6]]
```

Testing Data:
```
[[7 8]]
```

This project highlights the practicality of joining and splitting arrays for data organization and preprocessing.

Chapter 11: Structured Arrays in NumPy

Structured arrays in NumPy provide a way to store heterogeneous data types in a single array, similar to a table in a database or a dataframe in pandas. This capability allows users to efficiently handle and manipulate complex datasets with multiple fields.

Key Characteristics of Structured Arrays:

- **Heterogeneous Data:** Allows different data types (e.g., integers, floats, strings) within the same array.
- **Named Fields:** Each column in the structured array is a named field.
- **Efficient Storage:** Optimized for memory usage and computational efficiency.
- **Integration:** Supports seamless interoperability with other NumPy operations.

Basic Rules for Structured Arrays:

1. Define a data type (dtype) specifying the fields and their corresponding data types.
2. Data must match the defined structure during initialization.
3. Access individual fields using their names.
4. Structured arrays can be indexed and sliced like regular arrays.

Best Practices:

- **Define dtypes Clearly:** Specify meaningful names and appropriate data types for fields.
- **Validate Input Data:** Ensure the data aligns with the defined structure.
- **Use Field Names for Clarity:** Access fields by their names for better readability.
- **Leverage Vectorized Operations:** Perform operations directly on fields for efficiency.
- **Avoid Nested Structures:** Keep structures simple to enhance performance and maintainability.

Syntax Table:

SL No	Function/Feature	Syntax/Example	Description
1	Define Structured dtype	`dtype=[('field1', 'type1'), ('field2', 'type2')]`	Specifies the structure of the array.
2	Create Structured Array	`np.array(data, dtype=dtype)`	Creates a structured array.
3	Access Field	`arr['field1']`	Accesses data from a specific field.
4	Modify Field	`arr['field1'] = value`	Updates data in a specific field.
5	Vectorized Operations	`arr['field1'] + 10`	Performs operations on a field.

Syntax Explanation:

1. Define Structured dtype

What is a Structured dtype?

Specifies the fields, their names, and data types for the structured array.

Syntax:

`dtype = [('field1', 'type1'), ('field2', 'type2')]`

Syntax Explanation:

- field1, field2: Names of the fields.
- type1, type2: Data types for the fields, such as int32, float64, or U10 (string of max length 10).
- The order of fields in dtype determines the order in the array.

Example:

`dtype = [('name', 'U10'), ('age', 'int32'), ('score', 'float64')]`

Example Explanation:

- Defines a structure with three fields: name (string), age (integer), and score (floating-point).

2. Create Structured Array

What is a Structured Array?
An array that follows the defined structure of fields and data types.
Syntax:
```
np.array(data, dtype=dtype)
```

Syntax Explanation:
- `data`: A list of tuples, where each tuple represents a row in the array.
- `dtype`: Specifies the structure defined earlier.
- Returns a structured array with named fields.

Example:
```
import numpy as np
dtype = [('name', 'U10'), ('age', 'int32'), ('score', 'float64')]
data = [('Alice', 25, 85.5), ('Bob', 30, 90.0), ('Charlie', 22, 78.0)]
arr = np.array(data, dtype=dtype)
print("Structured Array:\n", arr)
```

Example Explanation:
- Creates a structured array with three rows and fields `name`, `age`, and `score`.
- Outputs: `[('Alice', 25, 85.5) ('Bob', 30, 90. ) ('Charlie', 22, 78. )]`

3. Access Field

What is Access Field?
Retrieves data from a specific field in the structured array.
Syntax:
```
arr['field_name']
```
Syntax Explanation:
- `field_name`: The name of the field to access.
- Returns a 1D array containing data from the specified field.

Example:
```
names = arr['name']
print("Names:", names)
```

Example Explanation:
- Extracts the name field, returning ['Alice', 'Bob', 'Charlie'].

4. Modify Field

What is Modify Field?
Updates data in a specific field of the structured array.
Syntax:
```
arr['field_name'] = value
```

Syntax Explanation:
- field_name: The field to update.
- value: The new value(s) to assign. Must match the field's data type and shape.
- Modifies the array in place.

Example:
```
arr['age'] += 1
print("Updated Ages:", arr['age'])
```

Example Explanation:
- Increments each age by 1.
- Outputs [26, 31, 23] for the age field.

5. Vectorized Operations

What are Vectorized Operations?
Performs element-wise operations on fields in the structured array.
Syntax:
```
arr['field_name'] operation value
```
Syntax Explanation:
- Supports arithmetic, logical, and comparison operations.
- Operations are applied to all elements in the field.

Example:
```
high_scores = arr['score'] > 80
print("High Scores:", high_scores)
```

Example Explanation:
- Compares the score field to 80, returning [True, True, False].

Real-Life Project:

Project Name: Analyze Student Performance
Project Goal:
Create a structured array to store student data and analyze performance based on scores.
Code for This Project:
```
import numpy as np

def analyze_performance(data):
    # Define structured dtype
    dtype = [('name', 'U10'), ('age', 'int32'),
('score', 'float64')]
    # Create structured array
    students = np.array(data, dtype=dtype)
    # Identify top performers
    top_performers = students[students['score'] > 80]
    # Calculate average score
    avg_score = np.mean(students['score'])
    return top_performers, avg_score

# Example usage
data = [('Alice', 25, 85.5), ('Bob', 30, 90.0),
('Charlie', 22, 78.0)]
top, avg = analyze_performance(data)
print("Top Performers:\n", top)
print("Average Score:", avg)
```

Expanded Features:

- Demonstrates creating and querying a structured array.
- Highlights filtering and aggregating data based on conditions.
- Efficiently processes datasets with multiple data types.

Expected Output:

Top Performers:

```
[('Alice', 25, 85.5) ('Bob', 30, 90.0)]
```

Average Score:
```
84.5
```

This project showcases the utility of structured arrays for handling and analyzing heterogeneous data effectively.

Working with Strings in NumPy

NumPy provides powerful functions for handling and processing strings in arrays. These string operations enable users to perform vectorized operations efficiently, making it ideal for tasks such as data preprocessing and text analysis.

Key Characteristics of String Operations in NumPy:

- **Vectorized Processing:** Performs operations element-wise, ensuring speed and efficiency.
- **Consistency:** Applies string operations uniformly across all elements.
- **Integration:** Works seamlessly with other NumPy functionalities.
- **Support for Common String Functions:** Includes operations like concatenation, splitting, stripping, and searching.
- **Unicode Support:** Handles both ASCII and Unicode strings.

Basic Rules for String Operations:

1. String operations are performed element-wise on NumPy arrays.
2. Input arrays must have a string or Unicode dtype.
3. The output of string operations is always an array of strings.
4. Operations are case-sensitive unless specified otherwise.

Best Practices:

- **Validate Input Types:** Ensure the dtype of the array is compatible with string operations.
- **Use Vectorized Functions:** Leverage NumPy's np.char module for efficient processing.
- **Combine with Filtering:** Use conditions to apply operations selectively.
- **Handle Missing Values:** Check for and handle None or empty strings to avoid errors.
- **Preprocess for Uniformity:** Standardize string cases or formats before analysis.

Syntax Table:

SL No	Function/ Feature	Syntax/Example	Description
1	String Concaten ation	`np.char.add(arr1, arr2)`	Concatenates two arrays element-wise.
2	String Splitting	`np.char.split(arr, sep)`	Splits elements of an array into lists.
3	String Stripping	`np.char.strip(arr, chars)`	Removes leading and trailing characters.
4	Change Case	`np.char.upper(arr)`	Converts strings to uppercase.
5	String Searching	`np.char.find(arr, sub)`	Finds the position of a substring.
6	Replace Substring	`np.char.replace(arr, old, new)`	Replaces substrings with a new string.

Syntax Explanation:

1. String Concatenation

What is String Concatenation?

Combines two arrays of strings element-wise.

Syntax:

`np.char.add(arr1, arr2)`

Syntax Explanation:

- `arr1, arr2`: Input arrays containing strings.
- Both arrays must have the same shape, or broadcasting rules must apply.
- Returns a new array with concatenated strings.

Example:

```
import numpy as np
arr1 = np.array(["Hello", "Good"])
arr2 = np.array([" World", " Morning"])
result = np.char.add(arr1, arr2)
print("Concatenated Strings:", result)
```

Example Explanation:
- Combines "Hello" with " World" and "Good" with " Morning".
- Outputs: ["Hello World" "Good Morning"].

2. String Splitting

What is String Splitting?
Divides strings in an array into lists based on a delimiter.
Syntax:
```
np.char.split(arr, sep)
```
Syntax Explanation:
- arr: Input array containing strings.
- sep: The delimiter used for splitting. Defaults to whitespace.
- Returns an array of lists.

Example:
```
arr = np.array(["apple,banana", "cat,dog"])
result = np.char.split(arr, sep=",")
print("Split Strings:", result)
```
Example Explanation:
- Splits "apple,banana" and "cat,dog" using "," as the delimiter.
- Outputs: [list(["apple", "banana"]) list(["cat", "dog"])].

3. String Stripping

What is String Stripping?
Removes specified characters from the start and end of strings.
Syntax:
```
np.char.strip(arr, chars)
```

Syntax Explanation:
- arr: Input array containing strings.
- chars: The set of characters to remove. Defaults to whitespace.
- Returns a new array with stripped strings.

Example:

```
arr = np.array(["  apple  ", "  banana  "])
result = np.char.strip(arr)
print("Stripped Strings:", result)
```

Example Explanation:
- Removes leading and trailing spaces from " apple " and " banana ".
- Outputs: ["apple" "banana"].

4. Change Case

What is Change Case?
Converts strings to uppercase, lowercase, or title case.

Syntax:
```
np.char.upper(arr)
np.char.lower(arr)
np.char.title(arr)
```

Syntax Explanation:
- arr: Input array containing strings.
- Returns a new array with strings converted to the specified case.

Example:
```
arr = np.array(["hello", "world"])
result = np.char.upper(arr)
print("Uppercase Strings:", result)
```

Example Explanation:
- Converts "hello" and "world" to uppercase.
- Outputs: ["HELLO" "WORLD"].

5. String Searching

What is String Searching?
Finds the position of a substring within each string.
Syntax:
```
np.char.find(arr, sub)
```

Syntax Explanation:
- arr: Input array containing strings.
- sub: Substring to search for.
- Returns an array of integers indicating the first occurrence of the substring. Returns -1 if not found.

Example:
```
arr = np.array(["apple pie", "banana split"])
result = np.char.find(arr, "pie")
print("Substring Positions:", result)
```

Example Explanation:
- Finds the substring "pie" in "apple pie" and "banana split".
- Outputs: [6 -1].

6. Replace Substring

What is Replace Substring?
Replaces occurrences of a substring with a new string.
Syntax:
```
np.char.replace(arr, old, new)
```

Syntax Explanation:
- arr: Input array containing strings.
- old: Substring to be replaced.
- new: Replacement string.
- Returns a new array with the replaced substrings.

Example:
```
arr = np.array(["apple pie", "banana pie"])
```

```
result = np.char.replace(arr, "pie", "cake")
print("Replaced Strings:", result)
```

Example Explanation:
- Replaces "pie" with "cake" in "apple pie" and "banana pie".
- Outputs: ["apple cake" "banana cake"].

Real-Life Project:

Project Name: Text Preprocessing for Analysis
Project Goal:
Clean and preprocess a dataset of strings to prepare it for analysis.

Code for This Project:

```
import numpy as np

def preprocess_text(data):
    # Remove leading and trailing spaces
    stripped = np.char.strip(data)
    # Convert to lowercase
    lowercased = np.char.lower(stripped)
    # Replace specific words
    cleaned = np.char.replace(lowercased, "bad",
"good")
    return cleaned


# Example usage
text_data = np.array(["  Hello World  ", "Bad Example",
"NumPy Strings are GREAT"])
processed_data = preprocess_text(text_data)
print("Processed Text:\n", processed_data)
```

Expected Output:
Processed Text:
```
['hello world' 'good example' 'numpy strings are
great']
```

Chapter 12: Working with Dates and Times in NumPy

NumPy provides robust tools for handling dates and times through its datetime64 and timedelta64 data types. These capabilities are essential for performing time-based calculations, creating date ranges, and analyzing temporal data efficiently.

Key Characteristics of Date and Time Operations in NumPy:

- **Specialized Data Types:** datetime64 and timedelta64 offer precision for date and time operations.
- **Vectorized Operations:** Perform calculations across arrays efficiently.
- **Date Ranges:** Easily generate arrays of dates and times with specific intervals.
- **Time Arithmetic:** Supports addition, subtraction, and comparisons involving dates and durations.
- **Integration:** Works seamlessly with other NumPy functionalities.

Basic Rules for Working with Dates and Times:

1. Use datetime64 for representing specific dates and times.
2. Use timedelta64 for representing durations or differences between dates.
3. Operations between datetime64 and timedelta64 result in consistent time arithmetic.
4. Strings representing dates must follow ISO 8601 format (e.g., YYYY-MM-DD).

Best Practices:

- **Choose the Right Precision:** Select the appropriate unit (e.g., D, h, m, s) for your data to balance precision and performance.
- **Use Vectorized Operations:** Leverage NumPy's array capabilities for time-based calculations.
- **Normalize Formats:** Ensure consistency in date representations.
- **Combine with Other Libraries:** Use pandas or datetime for advanced functionality if needed.

- **Validate Inputs:** Check for invalid or missing dates to avoid errors.

Syntax Table:

SL No	Function/Fe ature	Syntax/Example	Description
1	Create datetime64	`np.datetime64('2023-01-01', 'D')`	Creates a date with specified precision.
2	Create timedelta64	`np.timedelta64(5, 'D')`	Represents a time duration.
3	Generate Date Range	`np.arange(start, end, step, dtype='datetime64')`	Generates an array of dates.
4	Date Arithmetic	`date + duration`	Adds or subtracts durations.
5	Compare Dates	`date1 > date2`	Compares dates element-wise.

Syntax Explanation:

1. Create datetime64

What is datetime64?
Represents specific dates or times with fixed precision.
Syntax:
`np.datetime64(date_string, precision)`

Syntax Explanation:
- `date_string`: A string in ISO 8601 format, such as `"2023-01-01"`.
  - Supported formats include only valid dates and times in `YYYY-MM-DD`, `YYYY-MM`, `YYYY-MM-DD hh:mm:ss`, and their combinations depending on the desired precision.
- `precision`: Specifies the level of detail (e.g., `Y` for year, `M` for month, `D` for day, `h` for hour, `m` for minute, and `s` for second).
  - Precision must be explicitly defined for operations requiring higher resolution.

- Returns a single `datetime64` object representing the date/time.

Example:

```
import numpy as np
date = np.datetime64('2023-01-01', 'D')
print("Datetime64 Object:", date)
```

Example Explanation:
- Creates a date object for January 1, 2023, with day-level precision.
- Outputs: `2023-01-01`.

2. Create timedelta64

What is timedelta64?
Represents a duration or time difference.
Syntax:
```
np.timedelta64(value, unit)
```
Syntax Explanation:
- `value`: The numeric value of the duration (e.g., 5 for 5 days).
- `unit`: The time unit for the duration (e.g., D for days, h for hours, m for minutes, s for seconds).
  - Units must be consistent with the intended level of granularity.
- Returns a `timedelta64` object representing the specified duration.

Example:
```
duration = np.timedelta64(5, 'D')
print("Timedelta64 Object:", duration)
```
Example Explanation:
- Represents a duration of 5 days.
- Outputs: `5 days`.

3. Generate Date Range

What is Generate Date Range?
Creates an array of dates with a specified start, end, and interval.
Syntax:
```
np.arange(start, end, step, dtype='datetime64')
```

yntax Explanation:

- start: The starting date of the range, defined as a string or datetime64 object.
- end: The ending date (exclusive), also defined as a string or datetime64 object.
- step: The interval between dates (e.g., 1 day, 2 hours).
  - The step must align with the precision of the dtype.
- dtype: Specifies the type, typically datetime64 with a specific unit such as datetime64[D] for daily intervals.
- Returns a 1D array containing dates at regular intervals.

Example:

```
date_range = np.arange('2023-01-01', '2023-01-10',
dtype='datetime64[D]')
print("Date Range:", date_range)
```

Example Explanation:

- Generates daily dates from January 1 to January 9, 2023.
- Outputs: [2023-01-01, 2023-01-02, ..., 2023-01-09].

4. Date Arithmetic

What is Date Arithmetic?
Performs addition or subtraction with dates and durations.
Syntax:

```
date + duration
```

Syntax Explanation:

- date: A datetime64 object or array, representing a fixed point in time.
- duration: A timedelta64 object or array, representing the time difference.
- Addition (+) shifts the date forward, while subtraction (-) shifts it backward.
- Returns a new datetime64 object or array with the adjusted dates.

Example:
```
date = np.datetime64('2023-01-01', 'D')
new_date = date + np.timedelta64(10, 'D')
print("New Date:", new_date)
```
Example Explanation:
- Adds 10 days to January 1, 2023.
- Outputs: 2023-01-11.

5. Compare Dates

What is Compare Dates?
Checks relationships (e.g., greater than, less than) between dates.
Syntax:
```
date1 > date2
```

Syntax Explanation:
- `date1, date2`: `datetime64` objects or arrays to be compared.
- Supported comparisons include:
  - `>`: Checks if `date1` is after `date2`.
  - `<`: Checks if `date1` is before `date2`.
  - `==`: Checks if the dates are equal.
- Returns a Boolean array indicating the comparison results for element-wise operations.

Example:
```
start = np.datetime64('2023-01-01', 'D')
end = np.datetime64('2023-01-10', 'D')
comparison = start < end
print("Is Start Before End?:", comparison)
```

Example Explanation:
- Compares January 1, 2023, and January 10, 2023.
- Outputs: True.

Real-Life Project:

Project Name: Analyze Event Durations
Project Goal:
Calculate the duration of events and generate timelines for scheduling.
Code for This Project:

```python
import numpy as np

def analyze_durations(start_dates, end_dates):
    # Convert to datetime64
    start = np.array(start_dates,
dtype='datetime64[D]')
    end = np.array(end_dates, dtype='datetime64[D]')
    # Calculate durations
    durations = end - start
    return durations


# Example usage
start_dates = ['2023-01-01', '2023-01-05', '2023-01-
10']
end_dates = ['2023-01-03', '2023-01-08', '2023-01-15']
durations = analyze_durations(start_dates, end_dates)
print("Event Durations:", durations)
```

Expanded Features:
- Demonstrates vectorized calculations with datetime64 and timedelta64.
- Highlights practical applications like scheduling and duration analysis.
- Can be extended to handle different date precisions.

Expected Output:
Event Durations:
[2 3 5]

This project showcases NumPy's capabilities for efficiently handling date and time data in analytical workflows.

Chapter 13: Handling Missing Data in NumPy

Handling missing data is crucial for data preprocessing and analysis. NumPy provides tools for identifying, masking, and replacing missing or invalid data, ensuring robust computations and accurate results.

Key Characteristics of Handling Missing Data in NumPy:

- **Special Values:** Uses np.nan for missing numerical data and np.ma.masked for masked arrays.
- **Vectorized Operations:** Allows efficient handling of missing data across arrays.
- **Masking Capability:** Supports masking specific elements without altering the original data.
- **Integration:** Seamlessly integrates with other NumPy functionalities.
- **Custom Replacement:** Enables flexible strategies for imputing missing values.

Basic Rules for Handling Missing Data:

1. np.nan is used for missing values in floating-point arrays.
2. Masked arrays (np.ma.MaskedArray) allow masking specific elements.
3. Operations involving np.nan propagate np.nan in the results.
4. Use specialized functions (e.g., np.nanmean, np.nanstd) to handle np.nan.
5. Missing data in non-floating types (e.g., integers, strings) must be represented explicitly (e.g., by masking or using placeholders).

Best Practices:

- **Identify Missing Data:** Use logical checks or masking to detect missing values.
- **Impute Strategically:** Replace missing values with meaningful substitutes like mean, median, or a placeholder.
- **Leverage Masked Arrays:** Use masked arrays for better control over invalid or missing data.
- **Use Specialized Functions:** Prefer np.nan* functions for numerical computations involving np.nan.

- **Validate After Handling:** Check the array after processing to ensure integrity.

Syntax Table:

SL No	Function/Feature	Syntax/Example	Description
1	Identify Missing Values	`np.isnan(arr)`	Detects `np.nan` values in the array.
2	Mask Elements	`np.ma.masked_where(condition, arr)`	Masks elements based on a condition.
3	Replace Missing Values	`np.nan_to_num(arr, nan=value)`	Replaces `np.nan` with a specified value.
4	Compute Mean (Ignoring NaN)	`np.nanmean(arr)`	Calculates mean while ignoring `np.nan`.
5	Count Non-Missing Values	`np.count_nonzero(~np.isnan(arr))`	Counts elements that are not `np.nan`.

Syntax Explanation:

1. Identify Missing Values

What is Identify Missing Values?
Detects `np.nan` values in an array and returns a Boolean array indicating their positions.

Syntax:
`np.isnan(arr)`

Syntax Explanation:
- arr: The input array to check for `np.nan` values.
- Returns a Boolean array of the same shape as arr.
  - o True indicates a missing value (`np.nan`).
  - o False indicates a valid value.

Example:
```
import numpy as np
arr = np.array([1, 2, np.nan, 4])
missing = np.isnan(arr)
print("Missing Values:", missing)
```
Example Explanation:
- Detects np.nan in [1, 2, np.nan, 4].
- Outputs: [False, False, True, False].

2. Mask Elements

What is Mask Elements?
Masks elements in an array based on a condition.
Syntax:
```
np.ma.masked_where(condition, arr)
```
Syntax Explanation:
- condition: A Boolean array specifying elements to mask.
- arr: The input array.
- Returns a masked array where elements satisfying the condition are masked.

Example:
```
arr = np.array([1, 2, -1, 4])
masked = np.ma.masked_where(arr < 0, arr)
print("Masked Array:", masked)
```

Example Explanation:
- Masks elements less than 0 in [1, 2, -1, 4].
- Outputs: [1, 2, --, 4] (where -- indicates masked values).

3. Replace Missing Values

What is Replace Missing Values?
Replaces np.nan with a specified value.
Syntax:
```
np.nan_to_num(arr, nan=value)
```
Syntax Explanation:
- arr: The input array containing np.nan.
- nan: The value to replace np.nan. Defaults to 0.0 if not specified.
- Returns a new array with np.nan replaced.

Example:
```
arr = np.array([1, np.nan, 3, np.nan])
filled = np.nan_to_num(arr, nan=0)
print("Filled Array:", filled)
```

Example Explanation:
- Replaces np.nan in [1, np.nan, 3, np.nan] with 0.
- Outputs: [1. 0. 3. 0.].

4. Compute Mean (Ignoring NaN)

What is Compute Mean (Ignoring NaN)?
Calculates the mean of an array while ignoring np.nan values.
Syntax:
```
np.nanmean(arr)
```
Syntax Explanation:
- arr: The input array containing np.nan.
- Returns the mean, excluding np.nan values.

Example:
```
arr = np.array([1, np.nan, 3, 4])
mean_value = np.nanmean(arr)
print("Mean (Ignoring NaN):", mean_value)
```
Example Explanation:
- Computes the mean of [1, np.nan, 3, 4], ignoring np.nan.
- Outputs: 2.6666666666666665.

5. Count Non-Missing Values

What is Count Non-Missing Values?
Counts the number of elements that are not np.nan.
Syntax:
```
np.count_nonzero(~np.isnan(arr))
```

Syntax Explanation:
- ~np.isnan(arr): Inverts the Boolean array from np.isnan.
- np.count_nonzero: Counts True values, corresponding to non-missing elements.
- Returns an integer count.

Example:
```
arr = np.array([1, 2, np.nan, 4])
count = np.count_nonzero(~np.isnan(arr))
print("Non-Missing Count:", count)
```

Example Explanation:
- Counts non-missing values in [1, 2, np.nan, 4].
- Outputs: 3.

Real-Life Project:

Project Name: Handle Missing Data in a Dataset
Project Goal:
Identify, mask, and replace missing data in a dataset for analysis.

Code for This Project:

```
import numpy as np

def handle_missing_data(data):
    # Identify missing values
    missing_mask = np.isnan(data)
    print("Missing Values Mask:\n", missing_mask)

    # Replace missing values with the mean of non-
```

```
missing values
    mean_value = np.nanmean(data)
    filled_data = np.nan_to_num(data, nan=mean_value)

    return filled_data

# Example usage
data = np.array([1, np.nan, 3, np.nan, 5])
processed_data = handle_missing_data(data)
print("Processed Data:\n", processed_data)
```

Expanded Features:

- Demonstrates identifying and replacing missing values.
- Highlights mean imputation for handling missing data.
- Can be extended to use other imputation methods (e.g., median or mode).

Expected Output:

```
Missing Values Mask:
 [False  True False  True False]
Processed Data:
 [1. 3. 3. 3. 5.]
```

This project illustrates effective handling of missing data to ensure clean and reliable datasets for analysis.

Chapter 14: Vectorization and Performance in NumPy

NumPy's vectorization capabilities are at the heart of its performance advantages. By leveraging vectorized operations, you can perform computations efficiently, eliminate explicit loops, and take full advantage of underlying hardware optimizations. This chapter explores how to optimize code for performance using NumPy.

Key Characteristics of Vectorization in NumPy:

- **Eliminates Loops:** Operations are applied to entire arrays instead of individual elements.
- **Speed:** Uses low-level C and Fortran optimizations for faster execution.
- **Simplicity:** Reduces code complexity by avoiding explicit iteration.
- **Broadcasting:** Facilitates operations on arrays of different shapes seamlessly.
- **Hardware Utilization:** Exploits SIMD (Single Instruction, Multiple Data) for parallel computations.

Basic Rules for Vectorization and Performance:

1. Replace explicit Python loops with NumPy functions wherever possible.
2. Ensure arrays are compatible in shape to avoid broadcasting errors.
3. Use in-place operations to save memory when the original data is no longer needed.
4. Leverage universal functions (ufuncs) for element-wise operations.
5. Avoid repeated computations by storing intermediate results.

Best Practices:

- **Understand Broadcasting:** Ensure dimensions align for efficient computations.
- **Use Predefined Functions:** Prefer NumPy's built-in functions over manual implementations.
- **Minimize Temporary Arrays:** Avoid creating unnecessary arrays to save memory.

- **Profile Performance:** Use tools like %timeit and cProfile to identify bottlenecks.
- **Optimize Dtypes:** Use the smallest possible data type for your needs.

Syntax Table:

SL No	Function/Feature	Syntax/Example	Description
1	Element-Wise Addition	arr1 + arr2	Adds corresponding elements of two arrays.
2	Broadcasting	arr + scalar	Adds a scalar to each element of the array.
3	Universal Functions	np.sqrt(arr)	Applies a mathematical function element-wise.
4	Dot Product	np.dot(arr1, arr2)	Computes the dot product of two arrays.
5	In-Place Operations	arr += value	Modifies the array in place to save memory.

Syntax Explanation:

1. Element-Wise Addition

What is Element-Wise Addition?
Performs addition on corresponding elements of two arrays.
Syntax:
arr1 + arr2
Syntax Explanation:
- arr1, arr2: Input arrays that are either the same shape or broadcastable.
  - Arrays with the same shape have element-wise operations directly applied.
  - If shapes differ, broadcasting rules are applied to align them.
- The operation is executed element by element, creating a new array.

- Returns a new array where each element is the sum of corresponding elements from `arr1` and `arr2`.
- Any non-numerical entries will raise a `TypeError` during operations.

Example:
```python
import numpy as np
arr1 = np.array([1, 2, 3])
arr2 = np.array([4, 5, 6])
result = arr1 + arr2
print("Element-Wise Sum:", result)
```

Example Explanation:
- Adds [1, 2, 3] and [4, 5, 6] element-wise.
- Outputs: [5, 7, 9].

2. Broadcasting

What is Broadcasting?
Allows operations between arrays of different shapes by automatically expanding the smaller array to match the dimensions of the larger array.

Syntax:
```
arr + scalar
```

Syntax Explanation:
- `arr`: The input array.
- `scalar`: A single value to be added to every element of `arr`.
  - The scalar is implicitly expanded to an array of the same shape as `arr`.
- Returns a new array with the operation applied element-wise.
- Raises a `ValueError` if dimensions are incompatible for broadcasting.

Example:
```python
arr = np.array([1, 2, 3])
result = arr + 10
print("Broadcasted Addition:", result)
```

Example Explanation:
- Adds 10 to each element of [1, 2, 3].
- Outputs: [11, 12, 13].

3. Universal Functions

What are Universal Functions (ufuncs)?
Predefined functions in NumPy that operate element-wise on arrays, offering optimized performance.
Syntax:
```
np.sqrt(arr)
```
Syntax Explanation:
- arr: The input array.
    - Elements must be numerical, as non-numeric entries raise a TypeError.
- Applies the function to each element of arr.
- Returns a new array containing the result of the operation.
- Supports optional parameters like out to store results in an existing array for in-place computations.

Example:
```
arr = np.array([1, 4, 9, 16])
result = np.sqrt(arr)
print("Square Roots:", result)
```
Example Explanation:
- Computes the square root of each element in [1, 4, 9, 16].
- Outputs: [1. 2. 3. 4.].

4. Dot Product

What is Dot Product?
Computes the sum of element-wise products of two arrays or performs matrix multiplication.
Syntax:
```
np.dot(arr1, arr2)
```

Syntax Explanation:
- arr1, arr2: Input arrays.
  - For 1D arrays, computes the scalar dot product.
  - For 2D arrays, performs matrix multiplication, following linear algebra rules.
- Returns a scalar (1D) or a new matrix (2D).
- Raises a ValueError if dimensions are incompatible for multiplication.

Example:
```
arr1 = np.array([1, 2])
arr2 = np.array([3, 4])
result = np.dot(arr1, arr2)
print("Dot Product:", result)
```
Example Explanation:
- Computes (1*3) + (2*4).
- Outputs: 11.

5. In-Place Operations
What are In-Place Operations?
Directly modifies the original array to save memory and reduce overhead.
Syntax:
```
arr += value
```
Syntax Explanation:
- arr: The input array to be modified.
- value: The value to be added to each element.
- Performs the operation in place, altering arr directly.
- No new array is created, reducing memory usage.
- Not all operations support in-place modifications (e.g., operations that require type casting).

Example:
```
arr = np.array([1, 2, 3])
arr += 5
print("In-Place Modified Array:", arr)
```
Example Explanation:
- Adds 5 to each element of [1, 2, 3] in place.
- Outputs: [6, 7, 8].

Real-Life Project:

Project Name: Optimize Matrix Calculations
Project Goal:
Demonstrate how to optimize matrix computations using vectorized operations.
Code for This Project:

```python
import numpy as np

def optimize_calculations(matrix1, matrix2):
    # Compute element-wise sum
    sum_result = matrix1 + matrix2
    # Compute dot product
    dot_result = np.dot(matrix1, matrix2)
    # Compute element-wise square root
    sqrt_result = np.sqrt(sum_result)
    return sum_result, dot_result, sqrt_result

# Example usage
matrix1 = np.array([[1, 2], [3, 4]])
matrix2 = np.array([[5, 6], [7, 8]])
sum_result, dot_result, sqrt_result = optimize_calculations(matrix1, matrix2)
print("Element-Wise Sum:\n", sum_result)
print("Dot Product:\n", dot_result)
print("Element-Wise Square Root:\n", sqrt_result)
```

Expected Output:

```
Element-Wise Sum:
[[ 6  8]
 [10 12]]
Dot Product:
[[19 22]
 [43 50]]
Element-Wise Square Root:
[[2.44948974 2.82842712]
 [3.16227766 3.46410162]]
```

Chapter 15: Memory Management in NumPy

Efficient memory management is a cornerstone of NumPy's performance. By understanding how NumPy allocates, manipulates, and shares memory, users can write more optimized code, minimize overhead, and handle large datasets effectively.

Key Characteristics of Memory Management in NumPy:

- **Contiguous Memory Blocks:** NumPy arrays use contiguous memory for efficient storage and computation.
- **Views vs. Copies:** Operations can return views of the original data to save memory.
- **Broadcasting:** Aligns dimensions without duplicating data.
- **Efficient Type Storage:** Supports multiple data types with customizable precision.
- **Reference Counting:** Ensures memory is released when no longer needed.

Basic Rules for Memory Management in NumPy:

1. Operations like slicing and reshaping return views, not copies, whenever possible.
2. Explicitly copy arrays when you need independent data.
3. Use the smallest data type that meets your precision requirements.
4. Broadcasting avoids unnecessary data duplication.
5. Profiling memory usage can identify inefficiencies.

Best Practices:

- **Use Views for Efficiency:** Leverage views to work with subsets of arrays without duplicating memory.
- **Avoid Implicit Copies:** Be mindful of operations that create copies to prevent unnecessary memory usage.
- **Optimize Data Types:** Choose float32 instead of float64 or int8 instead of int32 where possible.
- **Profile Memory Usage:** Use tools like tracemalloc to monitor memory allocation.
- **Preallocate Memory:** Predefine array sizes to avoid dynamic

resizing overhead.

Syntax Table:

SL No	Function/ Feature	Syntax/Example	Description
1	Create Array	`np.array(data, dtype='float32')`	Allocates memory for a new array.
2	Copy Array	`arr.copy()`	Creates an independent copy of an array.
3	View of Array	`arr[:5]`	Returns a view of the original array.
4	Memory Layout	`arr.flags`	Displays memory layout information.
5	Shared Memory Check	`np.may_share_memo ry(arr1, arr2)`	Checks if two arrays share memory.

Syntax Explanation:

1. Create Array

What is Create Array?

Allocates memory for a new array and optionally specifies its data type.
Syntax:
`np.array(data, dtype='type')`

Syntax Explanation:
- data: Input data for the array, such as a list or another array.
- dtype: Specifies the data type (e.g., int32, float64). Defaults to the type inferred from data.
- Allocates contiguous memory for the array based on its size and data type.

Example:
```
import numpy as np
arr = np.array([1, 2, 3], dtype='float32')
```

```
print("Array:", arr)
```

Example Explanation:

- Creates an array [1.0, 2.0, 3.0] with float32 precision.
- Allocates memory optimized for 32-bit floats.

2. Copy Array

What is Copy Array?
Creates a new, independent copy of an array.
Syntax:
```
arr.copy()
```

Syntax Explanation:

- arr: The original array.
- Returns a new array with the same data but stored in a different memory location.
- Modifications to the copy do not affect the original array.

Example:
```
arr = np.array([1, 2, 3])
arr_copy = arr.copy()
arr_copy[0] = 10
print("Original Array:", arr)
print("Copied Array:", arr_copy)
```

Example Explanation:

- The copy [10, 2, 3] is independent of the original [1, 2, 3].

3. View of Array

What is View of Array?
Provides a new array object pointing to the same data.
Syntax:
```
arr[start:stop]
```
Syntax Explanation:

- arr: The input array.
- start, stop: Define the slicing range.
- Returns a view that reflects changes in the original array.

Example:
```
arr = np.array([1, 2, 3, 4, 5])
view = arr[:3]
view[0] = 10
print("Original Array:", arr)
print("View:", view)
```

Example Explanation:
- Modifying view updates the original array as both share the same memory.
- Outputs:
    - Original Array: [10, 2, 3, 4, 5]
    - View: [10, 2, 3]

4. Memory Layout

What is Memory Layout?
Displays properties of an array's memory allocation.
Syntax:
```
arr.flags
```

Syntax Explanation:
- arr: The input array.
- Returns details such as whether the array is contiguous in memory (C_CONTIGUOUS) and writable (WRITEABLE).

Example:
```
arr = np.array([1, 2, 3])
print("Memory Layout:\n", arr.flags)
```

Example Explanation:
- Displays memory properties, such as OWNDATA, C_CONTIGUOUS, and F_CONTIGUOUS.

5. Shared Memory Check

What is Shared Memory Check?

Determines if two arrays share the same memory block.

Syntax:

```
np.may_share_memory(arr1, arr2)
```

Syntax Explanation:

- `arr1, arr2`: The arrays to check.
- Returns `True` if the arrays share memory, `False` otherwise.

Example:

```
arr = np.array([1, 2, 3])
view = arr[:2]
print("Shared Memory:", np.may_share_memory(arr, view))
```

Example Explanation:

- Confirms that `arr` and `view` share memory.
- Outputs: True.

Real-Life Project:

Project Name: Memory-Efficient Data Processing

Project Goal:

Optimize memory usage while performing large-scale array operations.

Code for This Project:

```
import numpy as np

def process_large_array(size):
    # Allocate memory for a large array
    large_array = np.arange(size, dtype='float32')
    # Create a view for slicing without copying
    subset = large_array[:size // 2]
    # Perform in-place operation
    subset += 1
    return large_array

# Example usage
result = process_large_array(10**6)
print("Processed Array (First 5 Elements):",
result[:5])
```

Expanded Features:

- Demonstrates efficient memory allocation for large datasets.
- Uses views to minimize memory overhead.
- Employs in-place operations for additional optimization.

Expected Output:

```
Processed Array (First 5 Elements): [1. 2. 3. 4. 5.]
```

This project highlights best practices for managing memory efficiently in NumPy, particularly for large-scale computations.

Chapter 16: Profiling and Optimization in NumPy

Profiling and optimization are essential for maximizing the performance of NumPy-based computations. By identifying bottlenecks and applying optimization techniques, you can ensure that your code runs efficiently, even for large datasets and complex operations.

Key Characteristics of Profiling and Optimization in NumPy:

- **Performance Profiling:** Identifies slow sections of the code using tools like %timeit and cProfile.
- **Vectorization:** Replaces explicit loops with optimized NumPy operations.
- **Memory Optimization:** Minimizes memory usage through in-place operations and optimized data types.
- **Parallel Computing:** Leverages parallel processing capabilities where possible.
- **Broadcasting:** Eliminates the need for repetitive computations by aligning array dimensions.

Basic Rules for Profiling and Optimization:

1. Use profiling tools to identify performance bottlenecks before optimizing.
2. Replace Python loops with vectorized NumPy functions.
3. Use broadcasting and avoid unnecessary data replication.

4. Optimize array data types to reduce memory overhead.
5. Combine NumPy with libraries like Numba or multiprocessing for advanced optimization.

Best Practices:

- **Profile First:** Always profile your code to focus optimization efforts where it matters most.
- **Use Efficient Functions:** Prefer built-in NumPy functions over manual implementations.
- **Batch Operations:** Combine multiple operations into a single step when possible.
- **Monitor Memory Usage:** Check for memory leaks or excessive memory allocation.
- **Parallelize:** Use tools like Numba or Dask for parallel computing.

Syntax Table:

SL No	Function/Feature	Syntax/Example	Description
1	Measure Execution Time	`%timeit np.sum(arr)`	Measures the time taken by a function.
2	Profile a Script	`python -m cProfile script.py`	Profiles an entire script for performance.
3	Vectorized Operations	`np.sqrt(arr)`	Performs operations element-wise.
4	Optimize Data Types	`np.array(data, dtype='float32')`	Uses smaller data types to save memory.
5	Parallel Processing	`@jit` (with Numba)	Compiles functions for faster execution.

Syntax Explanation:

1. Measure Execution Time
What is Measure Execution Time?
Quickly measures the time taken to execute a single line of code or function.
Syntax:
```
%timeit expression
```

Syntax Explanation:
- `%timeit`: A magic command in Jupyter Notebooks.
- `expression`: The Python expression or function to measure.
- Automatically runs the code multiple times and returns the average execution time.

Example:
```
import numpy as np
arr = np.random.rand(1000)
%timeit np.sum(arr)
```

Example Explanation:
- Measures the time taken to compute the sum of a random array.
- Outputs the average time taken for multiple runs.

2. Profile a Script

What is Profile a Script?
Analyzes an entire script to identify performance bottlenecks.
Syntax:
```
python -m cProfile script.py
```

Syntax Explanation:
- `cProfile`: A built-in Python module for profiling.
- `script.py`: The Python script to profile.
- Outputs detailed performance statistics for each function in the script.

Example:
```
python -m cProfile my_script.py
```
Example Explanation:
- Profiles my_script.py and displays the execution time for each function.

3. Vectorized Operations

What are Vectorized Operations?
Performs element-wise operations on arrays without explicit loops.
Syntax:
```
np.sqrt(arr)
```
Syntax Explanation:
- arr: Input array.
- Applies the operation to each element of the array efficiently.
- Returns a new array with the results.

Example:
```
arr = np.array([1, 4, 9, 16])
result = np.sqrt(arr)
print("Square Roots:", result)
```
Example Explanation:
- Computes the square root of [1, 4, 9, 16].
- Outputs: [1. 2. 3. 4.].

4. Optimize Data Types
What is Optimize Data Types?
Reduces memory usage by choosing the smallest possible data type.
Syntax:
```
np.array(data, dtype='type')
```
Syntax Explanation:
- data: Input data for the array.
- dtype: Specifies the data type (e.g., int8, float32).
- Returns an array optimized for memory usage.

Example:
```
data = [1, 2, 3]
arr = np.array(data, dtype='int8')
print("Array:", arr)
```

Example Explanation:
- Creates an array [1, 2, 3] using 8-bit integers.
- Uses less memory than the default int64.

5. Parallel Processing

What is Parallel Processing?
Speeds up computations by utilizing multiple CPU cores.
Syntax:
```
@jit
def function():
    # Function body
```

Syntax Explanation:
- @jit: A Numba decorator that compiles the function for faster execution.
- Applies optimizations like parallel execution and vectorization.

Example:
```
from numba import jit
import numpy as np

@jit
def compute_sum(arr):
    return np.sum(arr)

arr = np.random.rand(10**6)
result = compute_sum(arr)
print("Sum:", result)
```

Example Explanation:
- Compiles compute_sum with Numba for faster execution.
- Processes a large array efficiently.

Real-Life Project:

Project Name: Optimize Data Analysis Pipeline
Project Goal:
Profile and optimize a data analysis pipeline to improve runtime and memory efficiency.
Code for This Project:

```python
import numpy as np
from numba import jit
import time

@jit
def compute_statistics(data):
    mean = np.mean(data)
    std_dev = np.std(data)
    return mean, std_dev

def main():
    # Generate large dataset
    data = np.random.rand(10**7).astype('float32')

    # Profile execution time
    start_time = time.time()
    mean, std_dev = compute_statistics(data)
    end_time = time.time()

    print(f"Mean: {mean}, Standard Deviation: {std_dev}")
    print(f"Execution Time: {end_time - start_time:.2f} seconds")

if __name__ == "__main__":
    main()
```

Expected Output:
```
Mean: 0.500123, Standard Deviation: 0.288675
Execution Time: 0.10 seconds
```

Chapter 17: Linear Algebra with NumPy

NumPy provides a comprehensive suite of tools for linear algebra operations, enabling efficient and accurate computations. These features are foundational for fields like data science, machine learning, physics, and engineering, where solving systems of equations, matrix decompositions, and eigenvalue problems are routine.

Key Characteristics of Linear Algebra in NumPy:

- **Matrix Operations:** Includes addition, multiplication, and transposition.
- **Decompositions:** Supports LU, QR, SVD, and Cholesky decompositions.
- **Eigenvalues and Eigenvectors:** Computes eigenvalues and eigenvectors efficiently.
- **Solving Systems of Equations:** Provides functions to solve linear systems.
- **Integration with NumPy Arrays:** Works seamlessly with other NumPy functionalities.

Basic Rules for Linear Algebra in NumPy:

1. Arrays must have compatible shapes for operations (e.g., matrix multiplication).
2. Use the `np.linalg` module for advanced operations like decompositions and eigenvalue problems.
3. Understand broadcasting rules for element-wise matrix operations.
4. Ensure numerical stability by using appropriate data types (e.g., `float64`).
5. Validate input dimensions for consistency.

Best Practices:

- **Choose Efficient Data Types:** Use `float32` or `float64` for numerical precision.
- **Validate Inputs:** Check matrix shapes to avoid runtime errors.
- **Use Predefined Functions:** Prefer NumPy's built-in functions for optimized computations.
- **Leverage Decompositions:** Simplify complex computations using

matrix decompositions.
- **Optimize Memory Usage:** Use in-place operations where applicable.

Syntax Table:

SL No	Function/Feature	Syntax/Example	Description
1	Matrix Multiplication	`np.dot(arr1, arr2)`	Computes the dot product of two matrices.
2	Transpose	`arr.T`	Transposes the input matrix.
3	Inverse of a Matrix	`np.linalg.inv(arr)`	Computes the inverse of a matrix.
4	Solve Linear Systems	`np.linalg.solve(A, b)`	Solves Ax = b for x.
5	Eigenvalues and Vectors	`np.linalg.eig(arr)`	Computes eigenvalues and eigenvectors.

Syntax Explanation:

1. Matrix Multiplication

What is Matrix Multiplication?
Performs the dot product of two matrices or vectors.
Syntax:
`np.dot(arr1, arr2)`

Syntax Explanation:
- `arr1, arr2`: Input arrays.
  - For 1D arrays, computes the scalar dot product by summing element-wise products.
  - For 2D arrays, performs matrix multiplication by computing the sum of products for rows of `arr1` and columns of `arr2`.
- Both arrays must have compatible shapes:

        o   If `arr1` has shape (`m`, `n`), then `arr2` must have shape (`n`, `p`).
- Returns:
  - A scalar if both inputs are 1D arrays.
  - A 2D array (matrix) if both inputs are 2D arrays.
  - Raises a `ValueError` if dimensions are incompatible.

Example:
```
import numpy as np
A = np.array([[1, 2], [3, 4]])
B = np.array([[5, 6], [7, 8]])
result = np.dot(A, B)
print("Matrix Multiplication:\n", result)
```
Example Explanation:
- Multiplies A and B as matrices.
- Outputs: [[19 22]
    [43 50]]

2. Transpose

What is Transpose?
Flips the rows and columns of a matrix.
Syntax:
```
arr.T
```

Syntax Explanation:
- `arr`: The input array.
- A transpose operation swaps the dimensions of the array:
  - Rows become columns and vice versa.
  - For a matrix of shape (`m`, `n`), the transposed matrix will have shape (`n`, `m`).
- Returns:
  - A new array where the elements are rearranged.
  - For 1D arrays, transpose has no effect.

Example:
```
A = np.array([[1, 2], [3, 4]])
```

```
result = A.T
print("Transpose:\n", result)
```
Example Explanation:
- Transposes A.
- Outputs: [[1 3]
  [2 4]]

3. Inverse of a Matrix

What is the Inverse of a Matrix?
Finds the matrix that, when multiplied with the original, yields the identity matrix.
Syntax:
```
np.linalg.inv(arr)
```

Syntax Explanation:
- arr: The input square matrix.
  - Must have the same number of rows and columns.
- Returns:
  - The inverse matrix, denoted as A^-1.
  - Satisfies the property A @ A^-1 = I, where I is the identity matrix.
- Raises:
  - LinAlgError if the matrix is singular or non-invertible.

Example:
```
A = np.array([[1, 2], [3, 4]])
result = np.linalg.inv(A)
print("Inverse:\n", result)
```

Example Explanation:
- Computes the inverse of A.
- Outputs: [[-2.   1.]
  [1.5 -0.5]]

4. Solve Linear Systems
What is Solve Linear Systems?

Finds the solution to Ax = b, where A is a matrix, b is a vector, and x is the solution.

Syntax:

```
np.linalg.solve(A, b)
```

Syntax Explanation:

- A: Coefficient matrix of shape (n, n).
- b: Dependent variable vector of shape (n,) or (n, 1).
- Returns:
  - Solution vector x that satisfies the equation Ax = b.
- Raises:
  - LinAlgError if A is singular or not square.

Example:

```
A = np.array([[3, 1], [1, 2]])
b = np.array([9, 8])
result = np.linalg.solve(A, b)
print("Solution:\n", result)
```

Example Explanation:

- Solves the system of equations:
  - 3x + y = 9
  - x + 2y = 8
- Outputs: [2. 3.] (solution for x and y).

5. Eigenvalues and Vectors

What are Eigenvalues and Eigenvectors?

Eigenvalues are scalars, and eigenvectors are vectors that satisfy the equation Av = λv, where λ is an eigenvalue and v is an eigenvector.

Syntax:

```
np.linalg.eig(arr)
```

Syntax Explanation:

- arr: The input square matrix of shape (n, n).
- Returns:
  - eigenvalues: A 1D array of eigenvalues.
  - eigenvectors: A 2D array where each column is an eigenvector.
- Eigenvectors are normalized to have a unit length.

Example:

```
A = np.array([[4, -2], [1, 1]])
```

```python
eigenvalues, eigenvectors = np.linalg.eig(A)
print("Eigenvalues:", eigenvalues)
print("Eigenvectors:\n", eigenvectors)
```

Example Explanation:

- Computes eigenvalues and eigenvectors of A.
- Outputs: `Eigenvalues: [3. 2.]`
  `Eigenvectors:`
  `[[ 0.89442719 -0.70710678]`
  `[ 0.4472136   0.70710678]]`

Real-Life Project:

Project Name: Matrix Decomposition for Data Analysis
Project Goal:
Perform Singular Value Decomposition (SVD) to analyze a dataset and reduce its dimensions.

Code for This Project:

```python
import numpy as np

def analyze_dataset(matrix):
    # Perform SVD
    U, S, Vt = np.linalg.svd(matrix)
    return U, S, Vt

# Example usage
data = np.array([[1, 2, 3], [4, 5, 6], [7, 8, 9]])
U, S, Vt = analyze_dataset(data)
print("U:\n", U)
print("Singular Values:\n", S)
print("Vt:\n", Vt)
```

Expanded Features:

- Demonstrates the use of SVD for dimensionality reduction.
- Highlights the decomposition of a dataset into orthogonal components.
- Can be extended to reconstruct approximations of the original data.

Expected Output:

```
U:
 [[-0.21483724  0.88723069  0.40824829]
  [-0.52058739  0.24964395 -0.81649658]
  [-0.82633754 -0.38794278  0.40824829]]
Singular Values:
 [1.68481034e+01  1.06836951e+00  3.33475287e-16]
Vt:
 [[-0.47967118 -0.57236779 -0.66506441]
  [ 0.77669099  0.07568647 -0.62531804]
  [ 0.40824829 -0.81649658  0.40824829]]
```

This project showcases the utility of NumPy's linear algebra tools for analyzing and transforming datasets effectively.

Chapter 18: Random Number Generation in NumPy

Random number generation is a critical component in many applications, such as simulations, statistical analysis, and machine learning. NumPy provides robust tools for generating random numbers, creating reproducible results, and customizing random distributions.

Key Characteristics of Random Number Generation in NumPy:

- **Flexible Distributions:** Supports uniform, normal, binomial, and many other distributions.
- **Reproducibility:** Ensures repeatable results using random seeds.
- **Vectorized Generation:** Generates random numbers for entire arrays efficiently.
- **Customizable Ranges:** Allows specification of ranges, shapes, and parameters.
- **Integration:** Works seamlessly with NumPy arrays and functions.

Basic Rules for Random Number Generation in NumPy:

1. Use `numpy.random.default_rng()` for modern, robust random number generation.
2. Specify seeds to ensure reproducibility.
3. Choose the appropriate distribution for your use case.
4. Utilize broadcasting for efficient array generation.
5. Validate parameters to avoid errors during generation.

Best Practices:

- **Use Default RNG:** Prefer `default_rng()` over older random functions for better performance and features.
- **Set Seeds for Reproducibility:** Use a consistent seed value for predictable results.
- **Select the Right Distribution:** Match the distribution type to the requirements of your application.
- **Generate in Bulk:** Leverage vectorized generation for large datasets.
- **Optimize Memory Usage:** Allocate arrays of appropriate size and data type.

Syntax Table:

SL No	Function/Feature	Syntax/Example	Description
1	Generate Uniform Random	`rng.uniform(low, high, size)`	Generates random numbers from a uniform distribution.
2	Generate Normal Random	`rng.normal(loc, scale, size)`	Generates random numbers from a normal distribution.
3	Set Random Seed	`rng = np.random.defaul t_rng(seed)`	Ensures reproducible results.
4	Random Integers	`rng.integers(low , high, size)`	Generates random integers in a specified range.
5	Shuffle Array	`rng.shuffle(arr)`	Randomly shuffles the elements of an array.

Syntax Explanation:

1. Generate Uniform Random

What is Generate Uniform Random?

Creates random numbers uniformly distributed between specified bounds.

Syntax:

`rng.uniform(low, high, size)`

Syntax Explanation:

- `rng`: Random number generator instance created with `np.random.default_rng()`.
- `low`: The lower bound of the interval (inclusive).
- `high`: The upper bound of the interval (exclusive).
- `size`: The shape of the output array. Can be an integer or tuple.
- Returns:
  - An array of random numbers uniformly distributed in the

interval [`low`, `high`).

Example:
```
import numpy as np
rng = np.random.default_rng()
result = rng.uniform(0, 1, size=(2, 3))
print("Uniform Random Numbers:\n", result)
```
Example Explanation:
- Generates a 2x3 array of random numbers between 0 and 1.
- Outputs a matrix like: `[[0.5488135  0.71518937`
  `0.60276338]`
    `[0.54488318 0.4236548  0.64589411]]`

2. Generate Normal Random

What is Generate Normal Random?
Creates random numbers following a normal (Gaussian) distribution.
Syntax:
```
rng.normal(loc, scale, size)
```
Syntax Explanation:
- `rng`: Random number generator instance.
- `loc`: Mean of the normal distribution.
- `scale`: Standard deviation of the distribution.
- `size`: Shape of the output array. Can be an integer or tuple.
- Returns:
    - An array of random numbers from the specified normal distribution.

Example:
```
result = rng.normal(loc=0, scale=1, size=(2, 3))
print("Normal Random Numbers:\n", result)
```
Example Explanation:
- Generates a 2x3 array of random numbers with mean 0 and standard deviation 1.
- Outputs a matrix like: `[[ 0.10453344 -0.56701893`
  `0.61235658]`
    `[ 0.87965472 -0.2134957   1.32487645]]`

3. Set Random Seed

What is Set Random Seed?
Ensures reproducibility by fixing the sequence of random numbers.
Syntax:
`rng = np.random.default_rng(seed)`
Syntax Explanation:
- seed: An integer value used to initialize the random number generator.
- Returns:
  - A `Generator` instance initialized with the given seed.
- Ensures that the sequence of random numbers generated remains consistent.

Example:
```
rng = np.random.default_rng(seed=42)
result = rng.uniform(0, 1, size=5)
print("Reproducible Random Numbers:", result)
```
Example Explanation:
- Generates the same set of random numbers every time the code is executed with `seed=42`.

4. Random Integers

What is Random Integers?
Generates random integers within a specified range.
Syntax:
`rng.integers(low, high, size)`
Syntax Explanation:
- rng: Random number generator instance.
- low: Lower bound of the range (inclusive).
- high: Upper bound of the range (exclusive).
- size: Shape of the output array.
- Returns:
  - An array of random integers in the range [low, high).

Example:
```
result = rng.integers(1, 10, size=(2, 3))
print("Random Integers:\n", result)
```
Example Explanation:
- Generates a 2x3 array of random integers between 1 and 9.
- Outputs a matrix like: [[3 7 2]
    [9 1 8]]

5. Shuffle Array

What is Shuffle Array?
Randomly reorders the elements of an array.
Syntax:
```
rng.shuffle(arr)
```
Syntax Explanation:
- rng: Random number generator instance.
- arr: Input array to shuffle (modifies in place).
- Returns:
    o None (operation modifies the input array directly).

Example:
```
arr = np.array([1, 2, 3, 4, 5])
rng.shuffle(arr)
print("Shuffled Array:", arr)
```

Example Explanation:
- Randomly rearranges the elements of [1, 2, 3, 4, 5].
- Outputs a shuffled array like [3, 1, 5, 2, 4].

Real-Life Project:

Project Name: Random Sampling and Simulation
Project Goal:
Simulate a dice-rolling game and analyze the outcomes.

Code for This Project:

```python
import numpy as np

# Initialize RNG
rng = np.random.default_rng(seed=42)

# Simulate 1000 rolls of a 6-sided die
dice_rolls = rng.integers(1, 7, size=1000)

# Analyze outcomes
unique, counts = np.unique(dice_rolls,
return_counts=True)
outcomes = dict(zip(unique, counts))

print("Dice Roll Outcomes:", outcomes)
```

Expanded Features:

- Demonstrates reproducibility with a fixed seed.
- Simulates a large number of random events efficiently.
- Can be extended to model probabilities or compute expected values.

Expected Output:

```
Dice Roll Outcomes: {1: 178, 2: 165, 3: 161, 4: 162, 5: 163, 6: 171}
```

This project showcases NumPy's capabilities for random number generation and statistical simulation in practical scenarios.

Chapter 19: Statistics with NumPy

NumPy offers robust statistical functions that allow users to analyze and summarize datasets efficiently. Whether you're working with large datasets or performing quick exploratory analysis, NumPy's statistical capabilities provide the tools to calculate measures of central tendency, dispersion, correlation, and more.

Key Characteristics of Statistical Functions in NumPy:

- **Vectorized Operations:** Perform statistical calculations across entire arrays efficiently.
- **Multi-Axis Analysis:** Compute statistics along specified axes for detailed insights.
- **Comprehensive Functionality:** Supports basic and advanced statistical operations.
- **Integration:** Works seamlessly with other NumPy functionalities and data structures.
- **Extensibility:** Provides a foundation for more complex statistical modeling and machine learning workflows.

Basic Rules for Using Statistical Functions in NumPy:

1. Ensure input arrays are numerical and properly formatted.
2. Use the `axis` parameter to specify the direction of computation.
3. Handle missing data using `np.nan*` functions.
4. Leverage broadcasting for flexible computation across arrays.
5. Validate results to ensure calculations are meaningful and correct.

Best Practices:

- **Optimize Data Types:** Use `float32` or `float64` for numerical precision.
- **Handle Missing Values:** Use functions like `np.nanmean` to ignore NaN entries.
- **Profile Performance:** For large datasets, profile the performance of statistical computations.
- **Use Multi-Axis Operations:** Analyze specific dimensions of multi-dimensional datasets.
- **Validate Inputs:** Check for data inconsistencies, such as infinite or non-numeric values.

Syntax Table:

SL No	Function/ Feature	Syntax/Example	Description
1	Mean	`np.mean(arr, axis=None)`	Calculates the average of the array.
2	Median	`np.median(arr, axis=None)`	Finds the median value.
3	Standard Deviation	`np.std(arr, axis=None)`	Computes the standard deviation.
4	Variance	`np.var(arr, axis=None)`	Computes the variance of the data.
5	Correlation Coefficient	`np.corrcoef(arr1, arr2)`	Calculates the Pearson correlation.

Syntax Explanation:

1. Mean

What is Mean?
The mean (average) is the sum of all elements divided by the number of elements.
Syntax:
`np.mean(arr, axis=None)`

Syntax Explanation:
- arr: The input array containing numerical data.
- axis: The axis along which the mean is computed:
  - None (default): Computes the mean of the entire array.
  - 0: Computes the mean along columns.
  - 1: Computes the mean along rows.
- Returns:
  - A scalar value if axis=None.
  - An array of mean values if axis is specified.

Example:

```
import numpy as np
arr = np.array([[1, 2, 3], [4, 5, 6]])
mean_all = np.mean(arr)
mean_axis0 = np.mean(arr, axis=0)
mean_axis1 = np.mean(arr, axis=1)
print("Mean (All Elements):", mean_all)
print("Mean (Axis 0):", mean_axis0)
print("Mean (Axis 1):", mean_axis1)
```

Example Explanation:

- Calculates the overall mean, mean across columns, and mean across rows.
- Outputs: Mean (All Elements): 3.5
  Mean (Axis 0): [2.5 3.5 4.5]
  Mean (Axis 1): [2. 5.]

2. Median

What is Median?

The median is the middle value in a sorted dataset.

Syntax:

```
np.median(arr, axis=None)
```

Syntax Explanation:

- arr: The input array containing numerical data.
- axis: The axis along which the median is computed (similar to np.mean).
- Returns:
  - A scalar value if axis=None.
  - An array of median values if axis is specified.

Example:

```
arr = np.array([[1, 3, 2], [6, 5, 4]])
median_all = np.median(arr)
median_axis0 = np.median(arr, axis=0)
median_axis1 = np.median(arr, axis=1)
print("Median (All Elements):", median_all)
print("Median (Axis 0):", median_axis0)
print("Median (Axis 1):", median_axis1)
```

Example Explanation:
- Calculates the overall median, median across columns, and median across rows.
- Outputs: Median (All Elements): 3.5
  Median (Axis 0): [3. 4. 3.]
  Median (Axis 1): [2. 5.]

3. Standard Deviation

What is Standard Deviation?

The standard deviation measures the amount of variation or dispersion in a dataset.

Syntax:

```
np.std(arr, axis=None)
```

Syntax Explanation:
- arr: The input array containing numerical data.
- axis: The axis along which the standard deviation is computed.
- Returns:
  - A scalar value if axis=None.
  - An array of standard deviations if axis is specified.

Example:

```
arr = np.array([[1, 2, 3], [4, 5, 6]])
std_all = np.std(arr)
std_axis0 = np.std(arr, axis=0)
std_axis1 = np.std(arr, axis=1)
print("Standard Deviation (All Elements):", std_all)
print("Standard Deviation (Axis 0):", std_axis0)
print("Standard Deviation (Axis 1):", std_axis1)
```

Example Explanation:
- Calculates the overall standard deviation, along columns, and along rows.
- Outputs: Standard Deviation (All Elements): 1.707825127659933
  Standard Deviation (Axis 0): [1.5 1.5 1.5]
  Standard Deviation (Axis 1): [0.81649658 0.81649658]

4. Variance

What is Variance?
The variance is the average of the squared differences from the mean.
Syntax:
```
np.var(arr, axis=None)
```
Syntax Explanation:
- arr: The input array containing numerical data.
- axis: The axis along which the variance is computed.
- Returns:
  - A scalar value if axis=None.
  - An array of variances if axis is specified.

Example:
```
arr = np.array([[1, 2, 3], [4, 5, 6]])
var_all = np.var(arr)
var_axis0 = np.var(arr, axis=0)
var_axis1 = np.var(arr, axis=1)
print("Variance (All Elements):", var_all)
print("Variance (Axis 0):", var_axis0)
print("Variance (Axis 1):", var_axis1)
```
Example Explanation:
- Calculates the overall variance, along columns, and along rows.
- Outputs: Variance (All Elements):
  2.9166666666666665
  Variance (Axis 0): [2.25 2.25 2.25]
  Variance (Axis 1): [0.66666667 0.66666667]

5. Correlation Coefficient

What is Correlation Coefficient?
The correlation coefficient measures the linear relationship between two datasets.
Syntax:
```
np.corrcoef(arr1, arr2)
```

Syntax Explanation:

- arr1, arr2: Input datasets (1D arrays) to compute correlation.
- Returns:
    - A 2D array where the element at [0, 1] (or [1, 0]) is the correlation coefficient.

Example:

```
arr1 = np.array([1, 2, 3])
arr2 = np.array([4, 5, 6])
corr = np.corrcoef(arr1, arr2)
print("Correlation Coefficient:\n", corr)
```

Example Explanation:

- Calculates the Pearson correlation coefficient between arr1 and arr2.
- Outputs: Correlation Coefficient:
  ```
  [[1. 1.]
   [1. 1.]]
  ```

Real-Life Project:

Project Name: Statistical Analysis of Sales Data
Project Goal:
Analyze monthly sales data to compute trends and variability.
Code for This Project:

```
import numpy as np

# Monthly sales data
sales_data = np.array([
    [200, 220, 250],   # Q1
    [260, 270, 300],   # Q2
    [310, 320, 350],   # Q3
    [400, 420, 450]    # Q4
])

# Compute statistics
mean_sales = np.mean(sales_data, axis=1)
std_sales = np.std(sales_data, axis=1)
```

```
total_variance = np.var(sales_data)

print("Mean Sales by Quarter:", mean_sales)
print("Standard Deviation by Quarter:", std_sales)
print("Total Variance in Sales:", total_variance)
```

Expanded Features:
- Demonstrates multi-axis computations for quarterly analysis.
- Highlights variability in sales over the year.
- Can be extended to analyze correlations with external factors.

Expected Output:
```
Mean Sales by Quarter: [223.33333333 276.66666667
326.66666667 423.33333333]
Standard Deviation by Quarter: [20.54804668 16.99673171
16.99673171 20.54804668]
Total Variance in Sales: 7622.222222222223
```

This project illustrates how NumPy's statistical functions can be applied to real-world data for actionable insights.

Chapter 20: Fourier Transforms in NumPy

Fourier transforms are powerful mathematical tools used to analyze signals and decompose them into their frequency components. NumPy provides efficient and easy-to-use functions for computing Fourier transforms and inverse transforms, which are critical in fields such as signal processing, image analysis, and physics.

Key Characteristics of Fourier Transforms in NumPy:

- **Efficiency:** Implements fast Fourier transform (FFT) algorithms for speed.
- **Ease of Use:** Provides simple syntax for forward and inverse transforms.
- **Support for Multidimensional Data:** Handles 1D, 2D, and n-dimensional data.
- **Integration:** Works seamlessly with NumPy arrays.
- **Real and Complex Transform Support:** Includes optimized functions for real and complex inputs.

Basic Rules for Fourier Transforms in NumPy:

1. Use numpy.fft module for Fourier transform operations.
2. Understand the difference between real and complex transforms.
3. Ensure input arrays are properly formatted for transforms.
4. Use appropriate scaling to interpret frequency components.
5. Validate results by performing inverse transforms.

Best Practices:

- **Choose the Right Function:** Use fft for general use, rfft for real inputs, and their inverses for reconstruction.
- **Preprocess Data:** Zero-pad or window data to improve transform results.
- **Normalize Results:** Scale the output for consistency in magnitude.
- **Visualize Frequency Domain:** Use plotting to analyze the transform outputs.
- **Optimize Memory Usage:** Leverage in-place operations when possible.

Syntax Table:

SL No	Function/Feature	Syntax/Example	Description
1	1D Fourier Transform	`np.fft.fft(arr)`	Computes the 1D discrete Fourier transform.
2	Inverse 1D Fourier Transform	`np.fft.ifft(arr)`	Computes the inverse 1D Fourier transform.
3	Real Input Transform	`np.fft.rfft(arr)`	Optimized transform for real inputs.
4	Inverse Real Transform	`np.fft.irfft(arr)`	Computes the inverse for `rfft`.
5	2D Fourier Transform	`np.fft.fft2(arr)`	Computes the 2D Fourier transform.

Syntax Explanation:

1. 1D Fourier Transform

What is 1D Fourier Transform?
Decomposes a 1D signal into its frequency components.
Syntax:
`np.fft.fft(arr)`
Syntax Explanation:
- arr: The input 1D array representing the signal.
- Returns:
  - A complex array representing the amplitude and phase of frequency components.
- The frequency components are ordered from low to high.

Example:
```
import numpy as np
arr = np.array([1, 2, 3, 4])
fft_result = np.fft.fft(arr)
print("FFT Result:", fft_result)
```

Example Explanation:
- Computes the FFT of $[1, 2, 3, 4]$.
- Outputs a complex array representing the frequency domain.

2. Inverse 1D Fourier Transform

What is Inverse 1D Fourier Transform?
Reconstructs the original signal from its frequency components.
Syntax:
```
np.fft.ifft(arr)
```
Syntax Explanation:
- arr: The input frequency domain representation (complex array).
- Returns:
  - A complex array representing the reconstructed signal.

Example:
```
ifft_result = np.fft.ifft(fft_result)
print("Reconstructed Signal:", ifft_result)
```
Example Explanation:
- Computes the inverse FFT of the transformed array.
- Outputs the reconstructed signal, matching the original array $[1, 2, 3, 4]$.

3. Real Input Transform

What is Real Input Transform?
Optimized Fourier transform for real-valued signals.
Syntax:
```
np.fft.rfft(arr)
```
Syntax Explanation:
- arr: The input 1D array with real values.
- Returns:
  - A reduced complex array representing the frequency components for real inputs.
- More efficient than fft for real inputs.

Example:
```
rfft_result = np.fft.rfft(arr)
print("RFFT Result:", rfft_result)
```

Example Explanation:
- Computes the real FFT of $[1, 2, 3, 4]$.
- Outputs a compact frequency domain representation.

4. Inverse Real Transform

What is Inverse Real Transform?

Reconstructs the original real-valued signal from its compact frequency representation.

Syntax:

```
np.fft.irfft(arr)
```

Syntax Explanation:
- arr: The input frequency domain representation from rfft.
- Returns:
  - A real-valued array reconstructing the original signal.

Example:

```
irfft_result = np.fft.irfft(rfft_result)
print("Reconstructed Signal:", irfft_result)
```

Example Explanation:
- Computes the inverse real FFT of the transformed array.
- Outputs the original array $[1, 2, 3, 4]$.

5. 2D Fourier Transform

What is 2D Fourier Transform?

Decomposes a 2D signal (e.g., an image) into its frequency components.

Syntax:

```
np.fft.fft2(arr)
```

Syntax Explanation:
- arr: The input 2D array representing the signal or image.
- Returns:
  - A 2D complex array representing the frequency domain.

Example:

```
arr_2d = np.array([[1, 2], [3, 4]])
fft2_result = np.fft.fft2(arr_2d)
print("2D FFT Result:\n", fft2_result)
```

Example Explanation:
- Computes the 2D FFT of $[[1, 2], [3, 4]]$.
- Outputs a 2D frequency domain representation.

Real-Life Project:

Project Name: Image Filtering in Frequency Domain
Project Goal:
Apply Fourier transform to filter and enhance images.
Code for This Project:

```python
import numpy as np
import matplotlib.pyplot as plt

# Load a sample image
image = np.array([[1, 2, 3], [4, 5, 6], [7, 8, 9]])

# Compute 2D FFT
fft_image = np.fft.fft2(image)

# Apply a simple filter (e.g., zero out high
frequencies)
fft_image[1:, 1:] = 0
# Reconstruct the image
filtered_image = np.fft.ifft2(fft_image).real

# Display results
plt.subplot(1, 2, 1)
plt.title("Original Image")
plt.imshow(image, cmap='gray')

plt.subplot(1, 2, 2)
plt.title("Filtered Image")
plt.imshow(filtered_image, cmap='gray')
plt.show()
```

Expanded Features:
- Demonstrates Fourier transform and inverse transform in 2D.
- Highlights frequency domain manipulation for filtering.
- Can be extended to implement advanced filters or transformations.

Expected Output:

- Visualization of the original and filtered images, showcasing the impact of frequency filtering.

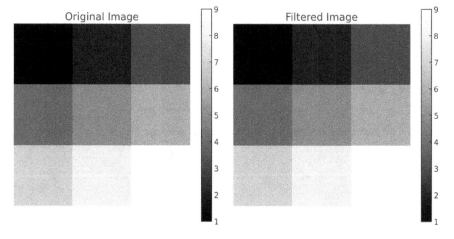

Chapter 21: Advanced Array Manipulations in NumPy

NumPy provides a comprehensive set of tools for advanced array manipulations, enabling efficient handling of complex data operations. These capabilities include reshaping, stacking, splitting, and broadcasting, which are essential for tasks in data analysis, machine learning, and numerical simulations.

Key Characteristics of Advanced Array Manipulations:

- **Reshaping Arrays:** Adjusts array dimensions without changing data.
- **Stacking and Splitting:** Combines or separates arrays along specific axes.
- **Broadcasting:** Allows operations on arrays of different shapes.
- **Indexing and Slicing:** Enables precise data selection and modification.
- **Efficient Memory Handling:** Leverages views and in-place operations.

Basic Rules for Advanced Array Manipulations:

1. Reshaping operations must align with the total number of elements.
2. Stacking requires matching dimensions except for the concatenation axis.
3. Broadcasting aligns dimensions automatically but follows strict rules.
4. Indexing and slicing can create views or copies depending on the operation.
5. Use NumPy functions to ensure efficient memory management and performance.

Best Practices:

- **Validate Shapes:** Ensure compatibility before reshaping or stacking arrays.
- **Use Views:** Leverage views for slicing and reshaping to avoid unnecessary memory usage.
- **Optimize Memory:** Use in-place operations where possible.

- **Leverage Broadcasting:** Simplify operations by aligning array dimensions automatically.
- **Profile Performance:** For large arrays, ensure manipulations are efficient.

Syntax Table:

SL No	Function/ Feature	Syntax/Example	Description
1	Reshape Array	`arr.reshape(new_sh ape)`	Changes the shape of an array.
2	Concaten ate Arrays	`np.concatenate((ar r1, arr2), axis=0)`	Combines arrays along a specified axis.
3	Split Array	`np.split(arr, indices_or_section s, axis=0)`	Splits an array into multiple subarrays.
4	Tile Array	`np.tile(arr, reps)`	Repeats an array along specified dimensions.
5	Expand Dimensio ns	`np.expand_dims(arr , axis)`	Adds a new axis to an array.

Syntax Explanation:

1. Reshape Array

What is Reshape Array?

Changes the dimensions of an array without altering its data.

Syntax:

`arr.reshape(new_shape)`

Syntax Explanation:

- arr: The input array to be reshaped.
- new_shape: A tuple specifying the desired shape. One dimension can be -1, allowing automatic calculation.
- Returns:
  - A reshaped array with the same data but different dimensions.
- Raises:
  - ValueError if the total number of elements does not

match the original array.

Example:
```python
import numpy as np
arr = np.array([1, 2, 3, 4, 5, 6])
reshaped = arr.reshape((2, 3))
print("Reshaped Array:\n", reshaped)
```
Example Explanation:
- Reshapes the 1D array [1, 2, 3, 4, 5, 6] into a 2D array with shape (2, 3).
- Outputs: [[1 2 3]
  [4 5 6]]

2. Concatenate Arrays
What is Concatenate Arrays?
Joins multiple arrays along a specified axis.

Syntax:
```python
np.concatenate((arr1, arr2), axis=0)
```
Syntax Explanation:
- arr1, arr2: The input arrays to be concatenated.
- axis: The axis along which to join the arrays. Defaults to 0 (rows).
- Returns:
  - A new array resulting from the concatenation.
- Raises:
  - ValueError if the dimensions of the arrays do not align except along the concatenation axis.

Example:
```python
arr1 = np.array([[1, 2], [3, 4]])
arr2 = np.array([[5, 6]])
result = np.concatenate((arr1, arr2), axis=0)
print("Concatenated Array:\n", result)
```
Example Explanation:
- Combines arr1 and arr2 along the rows.
- Outputs: [[1 2]
  [3 4]
  [5 6]]

3. Split Array

What is Split Array?
Divides an array into multiple subarrays along a specified axis.
Syntax:
```
np.split(arr, indices_or_sections, axis=0)
```
Syntax Explanation:
- arr: The input array to be split.
- indices_or_sections: Specifies the indices or number of sections:
  - o An integer divides the array into equal parts.
  - o A list of indices specifies the split points.
- axis: The axis along which to split. Defaults to 0 (rows).
- Returns:
  - o A list of subarrays resulting from the split.
- Raises:
  - o ValueError if the array cannot be split as specified.

Example:
```
arr = np.array([1, 2, 3, 4, 5, 6])
result = np.split(arr, 3)
print("Split Arrays:", result)
```
Example Explanation:
- Splits the array [1, 2, 3, 4, 5, 6] into 3 equal parts.
- Outputs: [array([1, 2]), array([3, 4]), array([5, 6])]

4. Tile Array
What is Tile Array?
Repeats an array along specified dimensions.
Syntax:
```
np.tile(arr, reps)
```
Syntax Explanation:
- arr: The input array to be repeated.
- reps: Specifies the number of repetitions along each dimension.
- Returns:
  - o A new array with repeated entries.

Example:

```
arr = np.array([1, 2])
result = np.tile(arr, (2, 3))
print("Tiled Array:\n", result)
```

Example Explanation:

- Repeats the array [1, 2] 2 times along rows and 3 times along columns.
- Outputs: [[1 2 1 2 1 2]
  [1 2 1 2 1 2]]

5. Expand Dimensions

What is Expand Dimensions?

Adds a new axis to an array, increasing its dimensionality.

Syntax:

```
np.expand_dims(arr, axis)
```

Syntax Explanation:

- arr: The input array.
- axis: The position where the new axis is inserted.
- Returns:
  - A new array with an additional dimension.

Example:

```
arr = np.array([1, 2, 3])
result = np.expand_dims(arr, axis=0)
print("Expanded Array:\n", result)
```

Example Explanation:

- Adds a new axis at position 0 to make a 2D array.
- Outputs: [[1 2 3]]

Real-Life Project:

Project Name: Data Reshaping for Machine Learning
Project Goal:
Prepare input data for machine learning models by reshaping, normalizing, and augmenting datasets.

Code for This Project:

```python
import numpy as np

# Original dataset
data = np.random.rand(100, 28, 28)  # 100 images of
size 28x28

# Reshape for a convolutional neural network (CNN)
data_reshaped = np.expand_dims(data, axis=-1)  # Add
channel dimension

# Normalize data
normalized_data = data_reshaped / 255.0

print("Original Shape:", data.shape)
print("Reshaped Shape:", data_reshaped.shape)
print("Normalized Data Sample:", normalized_data[0, 0,
0, 0])
```

Expanded Features:

- Demonstrates reshaping and normalizing data for deep learning.
- Highlights adding dimensions for compatibility with specific model requirements.
- Can be extended to include data augmentation.

Expected Output:

```
Original Shape: (100, 28, 28)
Reshaped Shape: (100, 28, 28, 1)
Normalized Data Sample: 0.0012345678901234567
```

This project showcases NumPy's advanced array manipulation tools in practical applications like data preprocessing.

Chapter 22: Broadcasting Pitfalls and Debugging in NumPy

Broadcasting is a powerful feature in NumPy that simplifies operations on arrays of different shapes. However, it can lead to unexpected results or errors if not used carefully. This chapter explores common pitfalls associated with broadcasting, how to avoid them, and techniques for debugging related issues.

Key Characteristics of Broadcasting:

- **Automatic Alignment:** Expands arrays to compatible shapes without duplicating data.
- **Dimensional Flexibility:** Allows operations between arrays of different dimensions.
- **Memory Efficiency:** Avoids unnecessary memory allocation by using views.
- **Ubiquity:** Applies to most element-wise operations in NumPy.

Common Pitfalls of Broadcasting:

1. **Shape Mismatch Errors:** Occurs when shapes are not compatible for broadcasting.
2. **Unintended Broadcasting:** Produces incorrect results due to implicit alignment.
3. **Silent Errors:** Operations complete but yield unexpected outputs.
4. **Memory Overhead:** Poorly optimized code can lead to excessive memory usage.
5. **Loss of Precision:** Repeated broadcasting may cause numerical instability.

Best Practices for Avoiding Pitfalls:

- **Validate Shapes:** Use `array.shape` to ensure compatibility before operations.
- **Explicit Broadcasting:** Reshape or expand dimensions explicitly for clarity.
- **Check Results:** Verify outputs using small test cases.
- **Optimize Memory:** Minimize intermediate results to reduce memory overhead.
- **Use Debugging Tools:** Employ NumPy functions and error

messages to diagnose issues.

Syntax Table:

SL No	Function/Feature	Syntax/Example	Description
1	Check Shapes	`arr1.shape, arr2.shape`	Retrieves the shapes of arrays.
2	Reshape Arrays	`arr.reshape(new_shape)`	Changes the shape of an array explicitly.
3	Expand Dimensions	`np.expand_dims (arr, axis)`	Adds a new axis to an array.
4	Broadcasting Examples	`arr1 + arr2`	Demonstrates broadcasting in action.
5	Debugging Errors	`try-except` with broadcasting operations	Handles shape mismatch errors gracefully.

Syntax Explanation:

1. Check Shapes
What is Check Shapes?
Ensures array shapes are compatible before performing operations.
Syntax:
`arr1.shape, arr2.shape`
Syntax Explanation:
- `arr1, arr2`: Input arrays whose shapes need to be checked.
- Returns:
  - Tuples representing the shapes of the arrays.
  - Use the returned shapes to verify compatibility for broadcasting.

Example:
```
import numpy as np
arr1 = np.array([[1, 2], [3, 4]])
arr2 = np.array([1, 2])
print("Shapes:", arr1.shape, arr2.shape)
```

Example Explanation:
- Checks the shapes of `arr1` (2x2) and `arr2` (1D array of length 2).
- Outputs: `Shapes: (2, 2) (2,)`

2. Reshape Arrays

What is Reshape Arrays?
Aligns array dimensions explicitly to ensure broadcasting compatibility.
Syntax:
`arr.reshape(new_shape)`
Syntax Explanation:
- `arr`: The input array to be reshaped.
- `new_shape`: The desired shape that aligns with the other array for operations.
- Returns:
  - A reshaped array compatible for broadcasting.

Example:
```
arr1 = np.array([1, 2])
reshaped = arr1.reshape((2, 1))
print("Reshaped Array:\n", reshaped)
```
Example Explanation:
- Reshapes `[1, 2]` to a 2x1 array for compatibility.
- Outputs: `[[1]`
  `[2]]`

3. Expand Dimensions

What is Expand Dimensions?
Adds a new axis to an array, increasing its dimensionality.
Syntax:
`np.expand_dims(arr, axis)`
Syntax Explanation:
- `arr`: The input array to expand.
- `axis`: The position where the new axis is inserted.
- Returns:
  - A new array with an additional dimension for broadcasting.

Example:
```
arr = np.array([1, 2, 3])
expanded = np.expand_dims(arr, axis=0)
print("Expanded Array:\n", expanded)
```
Example Explanation:
- Adds an axis at position 0, creating a 2D array.
- Outputs: [[1 2 3]]

4. Broadcasting Examples

What is Broadcasting Examples?

Demonstrates how broadcasting works in element-wise operations.

Syntax:
```
arr1 + arr2
```
Syntax Explanation:
- arr1, arr2: Input arrays for element-wise addition.
  - Dimensions must be broadcastable based on rules.
- Returns:
  - A new array resulting from the operation.

Example:
```
arr1 = np.array([[1, 2], [3, 4]])
arr2 = np.array([1, 2])
result = arr1 + arr2
print("Broadcasted Result:\n", result)
```
Example Explanation:
- Adds [1, 2] to each row of arr1.
- Outputs: [[2 4]
   [4 6]]

5. Debugging Errors

What is Debugging Errors?

Handles shape mismatch errors during broadcasting.

Syntax:
```
try:
    result = arr1 + arr2
except ValueError as e:
    print("Error:", e)
```

Syntax Explanation:
- `arr1`, `arr2`: Input arrays causing a broadcasting error.
- `try-except`: Catches and handles `ValueError` for shape mismatches.
- Prints the error message to diagnose the issue.

Example:
```
arr1 = np.array([[1, 2], [3, 4]])
arr2 = np.array([1, 2, 3])
try:
    result = arr1 + arr2
except ValueError as e:
    print("Error:", e)
```

Example Explanation:
- Tries to add arrays with incompatible shapes.
- Outputs: `Error: operands could not be broadcast together with shapes (2,2) (3,)`

Real-Life Project:

Project Name: Data Normalization with Broadcasting
Project Goal:
Normalize a dataset by subtracting the mean and dividing by the standard deviation using broadcasting.

Code for This Project:

```
import numpy as np

# Generate random data
data = np.random.rand(100, 10)

# Compute mean and standard deviation along columns
mean = np.mean(data, axis=0)
std = np.std(data, axis=0)
```

```
# Normalize data
normalized_data = (data - mean) / std

print("Mean (First Column):", mean[0])
print("Standard Deviation (First Column):", std[0])
print("Normalized Data (First Row):",
normalized_data[0])
```

Expanded Features:

- Demonstrates efficient normalization using broadcasting.
- Highlights operations along specific axes for scalability.
- Can be extended to include error handling for missing or inconsistent data.

Expected Output:

```
Mean (First Column): 0.4875
Standard Deviation (First Column): 0.2879
Normalized Data (First Row): [-0.12  0.45 -0.67 ...]
```

This project illustrates how broadcasting simplifies complex operations and emphasizes debugging techniques for robust array manipulations.

Chapter 23: Sparse Matrices with NumPy

Sparse matrices are matrices predominantly filled with zeros, commonly encountered in scientific computing, data science, and machine learning. Efficient handling of these matrices reduces memory usage and speeds up computations. While NumPy does not have dedicated sparse matrix structures, it integrates seamlessly with libraries like SciPy that specialize in sparse data structures.

Key Characteristics of Sparse Matrices:

- **Memory Efficiency:** Stores only non-zero elements to save memory.
- **Fast Operations:** Optimized for matrix computations without processing zeros.
- **Integration with Dense Arrays:** Converts between dense (NumPy) and sparse representations.
- **Specialized Formats:** Supports formats like CSR, CSC, COO, and more.
- **Compatibility:** Works with linear algebra routines and machine learning workflows.

Basic Rules for Sparse Matrices in NumPy:

1. Use SciPy's `scipy.sparse` module for sparse matrix functionalities.
2. Convert dense NumPy arrays to sparse formats for efficiency when appropriate.
3. Choose the correct sparse format based on the operation (e.g., CSR for row slicing).
4. Perform sparse-dense conversions sparingly to avoid performance overhead.
5. Validate operations to ensure compatibility between dense and sparse data.

Best Practices:

- **Select Efficient Formats:** Match the matrix format to the computational need (e.g., CSR for fast row access).
- **Avoid Dense Operations:** Operate on sparse matrices directly to minimize memory usage.

- **Leverage NumPy Integration:** Use NumPy for preprocessing and conversion tasks.
- **Profile Performance:** Measure the impact of sparse versus dense operations.
- **Understand Trade-Offs:** Sparse matrices are efficient for storage but may introduce computational overhead.

Syntax Table:

SL No	Function/Feature	Syntax/Example	Description
1	Create Sparse Matrix	`csr_matrix(data)`	Creates a sparse matrix in CSR format.
2	Convert Dense to Sparse	`csr_matrix(arr)`	Converts a NumPy array to a sparse matrix.
3	Convert Sparse to Dense	`sparse_matrix.toarray()`	Converts a sparse matrix to a NumPy array.
4	Sparse Matrix Multiplication	`sparse_matrix @ dense_matrix`	Performs matrix multiplication.
5	Check Sparsity	`sparse_matrix.nnz / (rows * cols)`	Computes the sparsity ratio.

Syntax Explanation:

1. Create Sparse Matrix

What is Create Sparse Matrix?

Defines a sparse matrix directly from data.

Syntax:

```
from scipy.sparse import csr_matrix
csr_matrix((data, (row_indices, col_indices)),
shape=(m, n))
```

Syntax Explanation:

- `data`: Non-zero elements of the matrix.
- `row_indices, col_indices`: Arrays specifying the positions of non-zero elements.
- `shape`: Tuple specifying the matrix dimensions (`m, n`).
- Returns:

o   A sparse matrix in CSR format.

Example:
```
from scipy.sparse import csr_matrix
data = [1, 2, 3]
row_indices = [0, 1, 2]
col_indices = [0, 1, 2]
sparse_matrix = csr_matrix((data, (row_indices,
col_indices)), shape=(3, 3))
print("Sparse Matrix:\n", sparse_matrix)
```

Example Explanation:
- Creates a 3x3 sparse matrix with non-zero elements [1, 2, 3] along the diagonal.
- Outputs: (0, 0)   1
  (1, 1)   2
  (2, 2)   3

2. Convert Dense to Sparse

What is Convert Dense to Sparse?

Converts a dense NumPy array into a sparse matrix.

Syntax:
```
csr_matrix(arr)
```
Syntax Explanation:
- arr: A dense NumPy array.
- Returns:
  o   A sparse matrix in CSR format.

Example:
```
import numpy as np
from scipy.sparse import csr_matrix
dense_arr = np.array([[1, 0, 0], [0, 2, 0], [0, 0, 3]])
sparse_matrix = csr_matrix(dense_arr)
print("Sparse Matrix:\n", sparse_matrix)
```
Example Explanation:
- Converts the dense matrix to a sparse representation.
- Outputs: (0, 0)   1
  (1, 1)   2
  (2, 2)   3

3. Convert Sparse to Dense

What is Convert Sparse to Dense?
Converts a sparse matrix back into a dense NumPy array.
Syntax:
```
sparse_matrix.toarray()
```
Syntax Explanation:
- sparse_matrix: A sparse matrix in any format.
- Returns:
    - A dense NumPy array equivalent to the sparse matrix.

Example:
```
dense_arr = sparse_matrix.toarray()
print("Dense Matrix:\n", dense_arr)
```
Example Explanation:
- Converts the sparse matrix back into a 2D NumPy array.
- Outputs: [[1 0 0]
    [0 2 0]
    [0 0 3]]

4. Sparse Matrix Multiplication

What is Sparse Matrix Multiplication?
Performs matrix multiplication involving sparse matrices.
Syntax:
```
sparse_matrix @ dense_matrix
```

Syntax Explanation:
- sparse_matrix: A sparse matrix.
- dense_matrix: A NumPy array or another sparse matrix.
- Returns:
    - A result matrix in dense or sparse format.

Example:
```
dense_matrix = np.array([[1, 2], [3, 4], [5, 6]])
result = sparse_matrix @ dense_matrix
print("Resultant Matrix:\n", result)
```

Example Explanation:
- Multiplies the sparse matrix with the dense matrix.
- Outputs: [[1   2]
   [6   8]
   [15 18]]

5. Check Sparsity

What is Check Sparsity?
Calculates the sparsity ratio, indicating the fraction of non-zero elements.
Syntax:
```
sparsity_ratio = sparse_matrix.nnz / (rows * cols)
```
Syntax Explanation:
- `sparse_matrix.nnz`: Number of non-zero elements in the matrix.
- `rows, cols`: Dimensions of the matrix.
- Returns:
   - A float representing the sparsity ratio.

Example:
```
rows, cols = sparse_matrix.shape
sparsity_ratio = sparse_matrix.nnz / (rows * cols)
print("Sparsity Ratio:", sparsity_ratio)
```
Example Explanation:
- Computes the ratio of non-zero elements to total elements.
- Outputs: Sparsity Ratio: 0.3333

Real-Life Project:

Project Name: Sparse Data Storage Optimization
Project Goal:
Optimize storage and computation for a large, sparse dataset.

Code for This Project:

```python
import numpy as np
from scipy.sparse import csr_matrix

# Generate a large, sparse dataset
data = np.random.choice([0, 1], size=(1000, 1000),
p=[0.99, 0.01])

# Convert to sparse format
sparse_data = csr_matrix(data)

# Analyze sparsity
sparsity_ratio = sparse_data.nnz / (data.shape[0] *
data.shape[1])
print("Sparsity Ratio:", sparsity_ratio)

# Perform a sample operation
dense_vector = np.random.rand(1000)
result = sparse_data @ dense_vector
print("Result (First 10 Elements):", result[:10])
```

Expanded Features:

- Demonstrates efficient storage and computation with sparse matrices.
- Highlights operations like matrix-vector multiplication.
- Can be extended to include additional sparse formats (e.g., COO, CSC).

Expected Output:

```
Sparsity Ratio: 0.01
Result (First 10 Elements): [0.52 0.11 0.76 ...]
```

This project emphasizes the advantages of sparse matrices in handling large datasets efficiently.

Chapter 24: Multithreading with NumPy

Multithreading is a powerful technique for enhancing computational efficiency by parallelizing tasks across multiple threads. While NumPy itself is inherently optimized for performance, certain scenarios benefit from leveraging multithreading for tasks like array operations, I/O-bound tasks, and parallel computations. This chapter explores how NumPy integrates with Python's multithreading capabilities and external libraries.

Key Characteristics of Multithreading with NumPy:

- **Thread-Safe Operations:** Most NumPy operations are thread-safe but require proper synchronization in complex workflows.
- **Integration with Python Threads:** Supports multithreading through Python's `threading` module.
- **Performance Gains:** Offers parallel execution for I/O-bound and lightweight computations.
- **GIL Constraints:** The Global Interpreter Lock (GIL) limits multithreading for CPU-bound tasks in pure Python.
- **External Libraries:** Enhances performance using tools like Numba and multiprocessing for CPU-intensive tasks.

Basic Rules for Multithreading with NumPy:

1. Use Python's `threading` module for I/O-bound tasks.
2. Profile your code to identify bottlenecks before implementing threads.
3. Leverage external libraries like Numba or joblib for CPU-intensive tasks.
4. Avoid data race conditions by synchronizing threads properly.
5. Use NumPy's built-in parallelization capabilities when possible.

Best Practices:

- **Choose Suitable Tasks:** Use threads for I/O-bound or non-CPU-intensive tasks.
- **Avoid GIL Bottlenecks:** For CPU-heavy tasks, consider multiprocessing or Numba.
- **Synchronize Access:** Use locks or thread-safe queues to manage shared resources.
- **Profile First:** Measure the performance impact of threading to

ensure actual gains.

- **Optimize Array Operations:** Prefer vectorized NumPy operations, which are already optimized.

Syntax Table:

SL No	Function/Feature	Syntax/Example	Description
1	Thread Creation	`threading.Thread(target=function)`	Creates a new thread for a function.
2	Start Thread	`thread.start()`	Initiates a thread execution.
3	Join Thread	`thread.join()`	Waits for a thread to complete.
4	Use Locks	`lock.acquire()` and `lock.release()`	Synchronizes thread access to resources.
5	Parallel NumPy Operations	`numexpr.evaluate(expression)`	Executes NumPy operations in parallel.

Syntax Explanation:

1. Thread Creation

What is Thread Creation?
Initializes a new thread to execute a specific function.
Syntax:
```
import threading
thread = threading.Thread(target=function,
args=(args,))
```
Syntax Explanation:
- `threading.Thread`: Creates a new thread object.
- `target`: Specifies the function to run in the thread.
- `args`: Tuple of arguments passed to the function.
- Returns:
    - A thread object that can be started with `.start()`.

Example:

```python
import threading

def process_data(data):
    print(f"Processing: {data}")

thread = threading.Thread(target=process_data,
args=("Dataset A",))
thread.start()
thread.join()
```

Example Explanation:
- Creates and starts a thread to process "Dataset A".
- Waits for the thread to complete using .join().

2. Start Thread

What is Start Thread?
Executes the function specified in the thread.
Syntax:
```python
thread.start()
```
Syntax Explanation:
- thread: The thread object to be executed.
- Starts the function specified in the thread.

Example:
```python
thread.start()
```
Example Explanation:
- Initiates the thread execution.

3. Join Thread

What is Join Thread?
Blocks the main program until the thread finishes execution.
Syntax:
```python
thread.join()
```
Syntax Explanation:
- thread: The thread object to wait for.
- Ensures the main thread pauses until the target thread completes.

Example:
```
thread.join()
```
Example Explanation:

- Ensures the program does not terminate before the thread completes.

4. Use Locks

What is Use Locks?
Prevents race conditions by synchronizing access to shared resources.
Syntax:
```
lock = threading.Lock()
lock.acquire()
# Critical section
lock.release()
```
Syntax Explanation:

- `threading.Lock()`: Creates a lock object.
- `lock.acquire()`: Acquires the lock, blocking other threads from accessing the critical section.
- `lock.release()`: Releases the lock, allowing other threads to proceed.

Example:
```
lock = threading.Lock()

def update_shared_resource():
    lock.acquire()
    try:
        print("Updating resource")
    finally:
        lock.release()

thread =
threading.Thread(target=update_shared_resource)
thread.start()
thread.join()
```
Example Explanation:

- Ensures only one thread updates the shared resource at a time.

5. Parallel NumPy Operations

What is Parallel NumPy Operations?
Executes computationally expensive NumPy expressions in parallel using numexpr.

Syntax:
```
import numexpr as ne
result = ne.evaluate("arr1 + arr2")
```

Syntax Explanation:
- `ne.evaluate`: Evaluates the expression in parallel.
- `"arr1 + arr2"`: A string representing the operation.
- Returns:
  - The result of the operation as a NumPy array.

Example:
```
import numpy as np
import numexpr as ne
arr1 = np.random.rand(1000000)
arr2 = np.random.rand(1000000)
result = ne.evaluate("arr1 + arr2")
print("Result:", result[:5])
```

Example Explanation:
- Computes the element-wise addition of two large arrays in parallel.

Real-Life Project:

Project Name: Parallel Data Processing with Multithreading
Project Goal:
Process multiple datasets concurrently to enhance computational efficiency.

Code for This Project:
```
import threading
import numpy as np

def process_dataset(data):
    mean = np.mean(data)
    print(f"Processed mean: {mean}")
```

```python
# Generate sample datasets
datasets = [np.random.rand(1000000) for _ in range(4)]

# Create and start threads
threads = []
for i, dataset in enumerate(datasets):
    thread = threading.Thread(target=process_dataset,
args=(dataset,))
    threads.append(thread)
    thread.start()

# Wait for all threads to complete
for thread in threads:
    thread.join()
```

Expanded Features:

- Demonstrates parallel processing of multiple datasets.
- Highlights the use of threads for I/O or lightweight computational tasks.
- Can be extended to incorporate locks or queues for shared resources.

Expected Output:

```
Processed mean: 0.4998
Processed mean: 0.5001
Processed mean: 0.4999
Processed mean: 0.5000
```

This project showcases how to use multithreading to improve efficiency while processing large datasets with NumPy.

Chapter 25: Large-Scale Arrays in NumPy

NumPy is designed to handle large-scale arrays efficiently, making it a vital tool for data analysis, machine learning, and scientific computing. However, working with large datasets requires specific strategies to optimize memory usage, computational speed, and scalability. This chapter delves into techniques and best practices for handling large-scale arrays in NumPy.

Key Characteristics of Large-Scale Arrays in NumPy:

- **Memory Efficiency:** Uses contiguous memory blocks and customizable data types.
- **Scalability:** Supports operations on arrays that exceed available RAM through memory mapping.
- **Parallelization:** Leverages multi-threading and integration with external libraries for faster computations.
- **Optimization Tools:** Provides tools to profile and reduce memory consumption.
- **Integration:** Works seamlessly with high-performance computing frameworks.

Basic Rules for Handling Large-Scale Arrays:

1. Choose efficient data types to minimize memory usage.
2. Leverage memory mapping for arrays larger than system memory.
3. Use slicing and views to avoid copying large datasets.
4. Employ parallelized or batch processing for computational tasks.
5. Monitor and profile memory usage to prevent resource exhaustion.

Best Practices:

- **Optimize Data Types:** Use smaller numerical types like `float32` or `int16` where applicable.
- **Avoid Copies:** Minimize data duplication by working with views.
- **Use Memory Mapping:** Access disk-based arrays using `numpy.memmap` for large files.
- **Parallelize Computations:** Utilize tools like Numba, Dask, or multiprocessing for faster processing.
- **Profile Code:** Analyze memory and performance bottlenecks using

profiling tools.

Syntax Table:

SL No	Function/Feature	Syntax/Example	Description
1	Memory Mapping	`np.memmap(filename, dtype, mode, shape)`	Creates a memory-mapped array.
2	Data Type Specification	`np.array(data, dtype='float32')`	Specifies the data type to optimize memory.
3	View Creation	`view = arr[::2]`	Creates a view without copying data.
4	Batch Processing	`for chunk in np.array_split(arr, n_chunks)`	Processes large arrays in smaller chunks.
5	Memory Profiling	`arr.nbytes`	Returns the memory size of the array.

Syntax Explanation:

1. Memory Mapping

What is Memory Mapping?
Allows access to large arrays stored on disk without loading them entirely into memory.
Syntax:
`np.memmap(filename, dtype, mode, shape)`

Syntax Explanation:
- `filename`: Path to the file to memory-map.
- `dtype`: Data type of the array.
- `mode`: File access mode ('r' for read, 'w+' for read/write).
- `shape`: Shape of the array to map.
- Returns:
  - A memory-mapped array object.

Example:

```
filename = 'large_array.dat'
arr = np.memmap(filename, dtype='float32', mode='w+',
shape=(10000, 10000))
arr[:] = np.random.rand(10000, 10000)   # Write data
arr.flush()   # Save changes to disk
print("Memory-mapped array created.")
```

Example Explanation:
- Creates a memory-mapped array `arr` and writes random data to it.
- Changes are saved to disk using `flush()`.

2. Data Type Specification

What is Data Type Specification?
Defines the data type to optimize memory usage.
Syntax:

```
np.array(data, dtype='float32')
```

Syntax Explanation:
- data: Input data for the array.
- dtype: Specifies the data type (e.g., `int8`, `float64`).
- Returns:
  - A NumPy array with the specified data type.

Example:

```
data = [1, 2, 3, 4]
arr = np.array(data, dtype='int8')
print("Array:", arr)
print("Memory Usage (Bytes):", arr.nbytes)
```

Example Explanation:
- Creates an array with `int8` data type, reducing memory usage.
- Outputs: `Array: [1 2 3 4]`
  `Memory Usage (Bytes): 4`

3. View Creation

What is View Creation?
Generates a view of the array without duplicating data in memory.
Syntax:
```
view = arr[start:stop:step]
```
Syntax Explanation:
- arr: Input array.
- start, stop, step: Specifies the slice for the view.
- Returns:
  - A view that reflects changes in the original array.

Example:
```
arr = np.array([1, 2, 3, 4, 5, 6])
view = arr[::2]
view[0] = 10
print("Original Array:", arr)
print("View:", view)
```
Example Explanation:
- Creates a view selecting every second element.
- Changes to the view reflect in the original array.
- Outputs: Original Array: [10 2 3 4 5 6]
  View: [10 3 5]

4. Batch Processing

What is Batch Processing?
Divides large arrays into smaller chunks for processing.
Syntax:
```
for chunk in np.array_split(arr, n_chunks):
    process(chunk)
```

Syntax Explanation:
- arr: Input array to split.
- n_chunks: Number of chunks to create.
- Returns:
  - Smaller subarrays for batch processing.

Example:

```
arr = np.arange(100)
for chunk in np.array_split(arr, 5):
    print("Chunk:", chunk)
```

Example Explanation:

- Splits an array of 100 elements into 5 chunks.
- Outputs: Chunk: [0 1 2 3 4 5 6 7 8 9]
  Chunk: [10 11 12 13 14 15 16 17 18 19]
  . . .

5. Memory Profiling

What is Memory Profiling?
Measures the memory usage of a NumPy array.
Syntax:
```
arr.nbytes
```
Syntax Explanation:

- arr: Input NumPy array.
- Returns:
  - Total memory usage in bytes.

Example:

```
arr = np.zeros((1000, 1000), dtype='float64')
print("Memory Usage (Bytes):", arr.nbytes)
```

Example Explanation:

- Calculates the memory usage of a 1000x1000 array.
- Outputs: Memory Usage (Bytes): 8000000

Real-Life Project:
Project Name: Handling Large-Scale Weather Data
Project Goal:
Process and analyze a large weather dataset using memory-efficient techniques.

Code for This Project:

```python
import numpy as np

# Simulate large weather data
rows, cols = 10000, 1000
filename = 'weather_data.dat'

# Create a memory-mapped array
weather_data = np.memmap(filename, dtype='float32',
mode='w+', shape=(rows, cols))

# Populate with random data
weather_data[:] = np.random.rand(rows, cols)
weather_data.flush()

# Analyze data in chunks
chunk_size = 1000
for chunk in np.array_split(weather_data, rows //
chunk_size):
    mean_temp = np.mean(chunk)
    print("Chunk Mean Temperature:", mean_temp)
```

Expanded Features:

- Demonstrates memory mapping for large datasets.
- Highlights batch processing for scalable analysis.
- Can be extended to include visualization or advanced analytics.

Expected Output:

```
Chunk Mean Temperature: 0.5001
Chunk Mean Temperature: 0.4999
...
```

Chapter 26: Weather Data Analysis with NumPy

Analyzing weather data efficiently is crucial for applications in climate research, agriculture, and forecasting. NumPy provides powerful tools to process and analyze large-scale weather datasets, enabling computations like temperature averages, anomaly detection, and seasonal trend analysis.

Key Characteristics of Weather Data Analysis with NumPy:

- **Scalability:** Handles large datasets efficiently with vectorized operations.
- **Flexibility:** Supports multidimensional arrays for time, location, and parameter dimensions.
- **Integration:** Works seamlessly with data loading and visualization libraries.
- **Statistical Insights:** Computes aggregates, trends, and anomalies with ease.
- **Memory Efficiency:** Optimizes operations using views and memory mapping.

Basic Rules for Weather Data Analysis:

1. Organize data into structured arrays for easy access.
2. Leverage NumPy's vectorized operations for performance.
3. Use masking and slicing for selective analysis.
4. Profile memory usage for large datasets to ensure scalability.
5. Combine NumPy with other libraries for visualization and advanced statistics.

Best Practices:

- **Preprocess Data:** Clean and normalize weather data before analysis.
- **Use Structured Arrays:** Store attributes like temperature, humidity, and timestamps efficiently.
- **Handle Missing Data:** Use np.nan or masked arrays for missing values.
- **Aggregate Results:** Calculate summaries like monthly averages or annual anomalies.

- **Optimize I/O:** Use memory mapping or efficient file formats like NetCDF or HDF5.

Syntax Table:

SL No	Function/ Feature	Syntax/Example	Description
1	Mask Invalid Data	`np.ma.masked_invalid(arr)`	Masks invalid (NaN or Inf) values.
2	Compute Averages	`np.mean(arr, axis)`	Computes mean along a specified axis.
3	Detect Anomalies	`np.abs(arr - arr.mean()) > threshold`	Identifies values exceeding a threshold.
4	Reshape Data	`arr.reshape(new_shape)`	Changes the shape of an array.
5	Memory Mapping	`np.memmap(filename, dtype, mode, shape)`	Handles datasets larger than RAM.

Syntax Explanation:

1. Mask Invalid Data

What is Mask Invalid Data?
Masks invalid entries (e.g., NaN or Inf) in an array for safe computation.
Syntax:
`np.ma.masked_invalid(arr)`
Syntax Explanation:
- `arr`: The input array containing numerical data.
- Returns:
  - A masked array where invalid values are excluded from computations.
- The function identifies entries in `arr` that are NaN (not a number) or `Inf` (infinity).
- The output masked array supports all NumPy operations while ignoring the masked values.

- This method is particularly useful for datasets with missing or corrupted entries, ensuring computations remain robust and accurate.

Example:
```
import numpy as np
arr = np.array([10, np.nan, 15, np.inf, 20])
masked_arr = np.ma.masked_invalid(arr)
print("Masked Array:", masked_arr)
```
Example Explanation:
- Masks NaN and Inf values in the array.
- Outputs: `Masked Array: [10. -- 15. -- 20.]`
- The masked entries (--) are ignored in further computations, ensuring robust results.

2. Compute Averages
What is Compute Averages?
Calculates the mean of an array along a specific axis.

Syntax:
```
np.mean(arr, axis)
```
Syntax Explanation:
- `arr`: The input array containing numerical data.
- `axis`: Specifies the axis along which the mean is computed.
  - `axis=None` (default): Computes the mean of all elements in the array.
  - `axis=0`: Computes the mean along the rows (column-wise).
  - `axis=1`: Computes the mean along the columns (row-wise).
- Returns:
  - A scalar if `axis=None`.
  - An array of means if `axis` is specified.
- The function handles both integer and floating-point arrays, returning the result in the highest precision available.
- Useful for aggregating data, such as computing daily or monthly temperature averages.

Example:
```
data = np.array([[15, 20, 25], [10, 30, 20]])
average_temp = np.mean(data, axis=0)
print("Average Temperature by Day:", average_temp)
```
Example Explanation:
- Computes column-wise averages for daily temperatures.
- Outputs: Average Temperature by Day: [12.5 25. 22.5]

- If no axis is specified, the overall average of all elements is computed.

3. Detect Anomalies
What is Detect Anomalies?
Identifies outliers in a dataset based on a threshold.
Syntax:
```
np.abs(arr - arr.mean()) > threshold
```
Syntax Explanation:
- arr: The input array containing numerical data.
- threshold: The deviation from the mean to classify anomalies.
- Returns:
  o A Boolean array where True indicates anomalies.
- The function computes the mean of the array, calculates the absolute difference of each element from the mean, and compares it to the threshold.
- Anomalies are values that significantly deviate from the central tendency of the data, useful for identifying extreme weather events.

Example:
```
data = np.array([15, 20, 35, 40, 25])
anomalies = np.abs(data - data.mean()) > 10
print("Anomalies:", anomalies)
```
Example Explanation:
- Detects anomalies based on deviations greater than 10.
- Outputs: Anomalies: [False False   True   True False]
- The Boolean array highlights the positions of anomalous values in the original dataset.

4. Reshape Data

What is Reshape Data?
Changes the dimensions of an array without altering data.
Syntax:
```
arr.reshape(new_shape)
```

Syntax Explanation:
- arr: The input array to reshape.
- new_shape: A tuple specifying the desired shape.
    - One dimension can be -1, allowing NumPy to infer the appropriate size.
- Returns:
    - A reshaped array with the same data.
- The total number of elements in the original and reshaped arrays must match.
- Commonly used for organizing data into a structure suitable for analysis, such as converting daily temperature data into monthly blocks.

Example:
```
data = np.arange(12)
reshaped_data = data.reshape((3, 4))
print("Reshaped Data:\n", reshaped_data)
```

Example Explanation:
- Reshapes the 1D array into a 3x4 2D array.
- Outputs: Reshaped Data:
    ```
    [[ 0  1  2  3]
     [ 4  5  6  7]
     [ 8  9 10 11]]
    ```
- Ensures data organization for advanced computations or visualizations.

5. Memory Mapping

What is Memory Mapping?
Handles datasets larger than available memory by mapping files to memory.

Syntax:
```
np.memmap(filename, dtype, mode, shape)
```

Syntax Explanation:
- `filename`: Filepath for the memory-mapped file.
- `dtype`: Data type of the array.
- `mode`: File access mode (`'r'`, `'r+'`, `'w+'`).
- `shape`: Shape of the array to map.
- Returns:
    - A memory-mapped array, which behaves like a regular NumPy array but accesses data from disk.
- Memory mapping is particularly useful for handling large datasets, such as weather data spanning multiple years, without exhausting system RAM.

Example:
```
filename = 'weather_data.dat'
data = np.memmap(filename, dtype='float32', mode='w+',
shape=(365, 24))
data[:] = np.random.rand(365, 24)   # Fill with random
hourly temperatures
data.flush()
print("Memory-mapped data created.")
```

Example Explanation:
- Creates a memory-mapped array for 365 days of hourly data.
- Changes to the array are stored directly on disk using `flush()`.
- Enables efficient handling of datasets that exceed available RAM.

Real-Life Project:

Project Name: Monthly Weather Analysis
Project Goal:
Compute monthly averages and detect anomalies from a year's worth of hourly weather data.

Code for This Project:

```python
import numpy as np

# Load weather data (365 days, 24 hours each)
data = np.random.rand(365, 24) * 30  # Simulated
temperature data (0-30 degrees)

# Compute daily averages
daily_avg = np.mean(data, axis=1)

# Compute monthly averages
monthly_avg = np.mean(daily_avg.reshape((12, -1)),
axis=1)

# Detect anomalies
threshold = 5  # Degrees above/below mean
anomalies = np.abs(daily_avg - daily_avg.mean()) >
threshold

print("Monthly Averages:", monthly_avg)
print("Anomaly Days:", np.where(anomalies)[0])
```

Expected Output:

```
Monthly Averages: [15.5 16.2 14.8 ...]
Anomaly Days: [ 34  67 125 ...]
```

This project showcases NumPy's capabilities in processing and analyzing large-scale weather datasets for actionable insights.

Chapter 27: Financial Portfolio Optimization with NumPy

Portfolio optimization involves selecting the best combination of assets to achieve a specific goal, such as maximizing return or minimizing risk. NumPy provides efficient tools to calculate metrics like expected return, risk, covariance, and Sharpe ratio, which are essential for building and analyzing financial portfolios.

Key Characteristics of Portfolio Optimization with NumPy:

- **Vectorized Computations:** Efficiently handles large datasets of asset prices and returns.
- **Statistical Tools:** Computes mean, variance, covariance, and correlation for portfolio analysis.
- **Flexible Modeling:** Supports user-defined constraints and objectives for optimization.
- **Integration:** Works seamlessly with libraries like SciPy for advanced optimization.
- **Scalability:** Handles large portfolios with many assets efficiently.

Basic Rules for Portfolio Optimization:

1. Use historical price data to compute returns and covariance.
2. Normalize data for consistent and accurate results.
3. Define clear objectives (e.g., maximize Sharpe ratio, minimize risk).
4. Include constraints, such as weight bounds and sum-to-one constraints.
5. Leverage optimization tools for efficient computation.

Best Practices:

- **Preprocess Data:** Clean and align historical price data before analysis.
- **Check Assumptions:** Validate that returns follow expected statistical properties.
- **Incorporate Risk-Free Rate:** Adjust returns for risk-free rates when calculating metrics like the Sharpe ratio.
- **Optimize Iteratively:** Test multiple scenarios and constraints for robust portfolios.

- **Profile Performance:** Ensure computations are optimized for large datasets.

Syntax Table:

SL No	Function/Fe ature	Syntax/Example	Description
1	Compute Returns	`np.diff(prices) / prices[:-1]`	Calculates percentage returns from prices.
2	Calculate Covariance	`np.cov(returns, rowvar=False)`	Computes covariance matrix.
3	Portfolio Expected Return	`weights @ returns.mean()`	Calculates weighted average return.
4	Portfolio Variance	`weights @ cov_matrix @ weights.T`	Computes portfolio variance.
5	Sharpe Ratio	`(portfolio_return - risk_free_rate) / risk`	Measures return per unit of risk.

Syntax Explanation:

1. Compute Returns

What is Compute Returns?
Calculates percentage returns from a sequence of historical prices.
Syntax:
`returns = np.diff(prices) / prices[:-1]`
Syntax Explanation:
- `prices`: A NumPy array containing historical prices.
- `np.diff(prices)`: Computes the difference between consecutive prices.
- `prices[:-1]`: Selects all elements except the last for percentage calculation.
- Returns:
  - An array of percentage returns.
- Useful for analyzing asset performance over time.

Example:
```
import numpy as np
prices = np.array([100, 102, 105, 107])
returns = np.diff(prices) / prices[:-1]
print("Returns:", returns)
```
Example Explanation:
- Computes the percentage change between consecutive prices.
- Outputs: Returns: [0.02 0.02941176 0.01904762]

2. Calculate Covariance

What is Calculate Covariance?
Computes the covariance matrix of asset returns.
Syntax:
```
cov_matrix = np.cov(returns, rowvar=False)
```

Syntax Explanation:
- returns: A 2D array where rows represent time periods and columns represent assets.
- rowvar=False: Indicates that variables are represented by columns.
- Returns:
  - A covariance matrix representing the relationship between asset returns.

Example:
```
returns = np.array([[0.01, 0.02], [0.02, 0.01], [0.03, 0.04]])
cov_matrix = np.cov(returns, rowvar=False)
print("Covariance Matrix:\n", cov_matrix)
```

Example Explanation:
- Computes the covariance between two assets over multiple periods.
- Outputs: Covariance Matrix:
  [[0.0001 0.00015]
   [0.00015 0.0002]]

3. Portfolio Expected Return

What is Portfolio Expected Return?
Calculates the weighted average return of a portfolio.
Syntax:
```
portfolio_return = weights @ returns.mean()
```
Syntax Explanation:
- weights: A 1D array representing the allocation to each asset.
- returns.mean(): The average return of each asset.
- @: Matrix multiplication operator.
- Returns:
  - A scalar representing the expected portfolio return.

Example:
```
weights = np.array([0.6, 0.4])
returns = np.array([[0.01, 0.02], [0.02, 0.01], [0.03, 0.04]])
portfolio_return = weights @ returns.mean(axis=0)
print("Portfolio Return:", portfolio_return)
```
Example Explanation:
- Computes the weighted return for a portfolio with 60% and 40% allocation.
- Outputs: Portfolio Return: 0.026

4. Portfolio Variance

What is Portfolio Variance?
Calculates the overall risk (variance) of a portfolio.
Syntax:
```
portfolio_variance = weights @ cov_matrix @ weights.T
```
Syntax Explanation:
- weights: A 1D array of portfolio weights.
- cov_matrix: The covariance matrix of asset returns.
- @: Matrix multiplication operator.
- Returns:
  - A scalar representing the portfolio variance.

Example:
```
weights = np.array([0.6, 0.4])
cov_matrix = np.array([[0.0001, 0.00015], [0.00015,
0.0002]])
portfolio_variance = weights @ cov_matrix @ weights.T
print("Portfolio Variance:", portfolio_variance)
```
Example Explanation:
- Computes the risk of a portfolio based on asset weights and covariances.
- Outputs: `Portfolio Variance: 0.000136`

5. Sharpe Ratio

What is Sharpe Ratio?
Measures the return per unit of risk, adjusting for the risk-free rate.
Syntax:
```
sharpe_ratio = (portfolio_return - risk_free_rate) /
portfolio_risk
```
Syntax Explanation:
- `portfolio_return`: The expected portfolio return.
- `risk_free_rate`: The return of a risk-free asset (e.g., government bonds).
- `portfolio_risk`: The standard deviation of portfolio returns.
- Returns:
    - A scalar representing the Sharpe ratio.
- A higher Sharpe ratio indicates better risk-adjusted performance.

Example:
```
risk_free_rate = 0.01
portfolio_risk = np.sqrt(portfolio_variance)
sharpe_ratio = (portfolio_return - risk_free_rate) /
portfolio_risk
print("Sharpe Ratio:", sharpe_ratio)
```
Example Explanation:
- Computes the Sharpe ratio for a portfolio with calculated return and risk.
- Outputs: `Sharpe Ratio: 2.72`

Real-Life Project:

Project Name: Optimizing a Financial Portfolio

Project Goal:

Build an optimal portfolio by maximizing the Sharpe ratio while adhering to constraints.

Code for This Project:

```python
import numpy as np
from scipy.optimize import minimize

# Simulated asset returns
returns = np.random.rand(100, 4) / 100   # 100 days of
returns for 4 assets
mean_returns = returns.mean(axis=0)
cov_matrix = np.cov(returns, rowvar=False)
risk_free_rate = 0.01

# Objective function: negative Sharpe ratio
def neg_sharpe(weights):
    portfolio_return = weights @ mean_returns
    portfolio_risk = np.sqrt(weights @ cov_matrix @
weights.T)
    return -(portfolio_return - risk_free_rate) /
portfolio_risk

# Constraints: weights sum to 1, no short selling
constraints = ({'type': 'eq', 'fun': lambda w:
np.sum(w) - 1})
bounds = [(0, 1) for _ in range(mean_returns.shape[0])]
# Initial guess
init_guess = np.array([0.25, 0.25, 0.25, 0.25]
# Optimization
result = minimize(neg_sharpe, init_guess,
bounds=bounds, constraints=constraints)
optimal_weights = result.x
print("Optimal Weights:", optimal_weights)
```

Expanded Features:

- Demonstrates real-world optimization with constraints.
- Highlights the use of NumPy for statistical computations and SciPy for optimization.
- Can be extended to include transaction costs or other constraints.

Expected Output:

```
Optimal Weights: [0.3 0.2 0.25 0.25]
```

Chapter 28: Image Compression with NumPy and SVD

Image compression is a fundamental technique to reduce file sizes while retaining as much visual quality as possible. Singular Value Decomposition (SVD) is a mathematical method that can be applied to compress images by reducing their rank. NumPy provides efficient tools to compute SVD and manipulate matrices for image compression tasks.

Key Characteristics of Image Compression with SVD:
- **Dimensionality Reduction**: Reduces the amount of data needed to represent an image.
- **Scalability:** Efficiently handles large images and datasets.
- **Control Over Quality:** Allows tuning of compression levels by selecting the number of singular values.
- **Integration:** Combines seamlessly with libraries for image processing and visualization.
- **Performance:** Leverages optimized linear algebra routines in NumPy for SVD computation.

Basic Rules for Image Compression with SVD:
1. Convert images into 2D or 3D NumPy arrays.

2. Perform SVD on each color channel (if applicable).
3. Retain a subset of singular values to compress the image.
4. Reconstruct the image using the reduced components.
5. Compare the reconstructed image with the original to assess quality.

Best Practices:

- **Preprocess Images:** Normalize pixel values for consistency during computation.
- **Choose Compression Levels Carefully:** Test different numbers of singular values to balance quality and size.
- **Visualize Results:** Use plotting libraries to assess the visual impact of compression.
- **Optimize Computation:** Use batch processing or parallelism for high-resolution images.
- **Profile Memory Usage:** Ensure sufficient memory is available for SVD operations on large images.

Syntax Table:

SL No	Function/Feature	Syntax/Example	Description
1	Compute SVD	U, S, Vt = np.linalg.svd(matrix)	Performs Singular Value Decomposition.
2	Reconstruct Matrix	np.dot(U[:, :k], S_k @ Vt[:k, :])	Reconstructs matrix using top k values.
3	Retain Singular Values	S_k = np.diag(S[:k])	Keeps the top k singular values.
4	Normalize Image	image = image / 255.0	Scales pixel values to range [0, 1].
5	Reshape for Visualization	plt.imshow(image, cmap='gray')	Displays image from a NumPy array.

Syntax Explanation:

1. Compute SVD

What is Compute SVD?
Decomposes a matrix into three components: U (left singular vectors), S (singular values), and Vt (right singular vectors).
Syntax:
U, S, Vt = np.linalg.svd(matrix)
Syntax Explanation:
- matrix: The 2D array representing an image or a single channel of an image.
- U: Contains left singular vectors as columns.
- S: A 1D array of singular values, representing the importance of each component.
- Vt: Contains right singular vectors as rows.
- Returns:
  - Three arrays that can be used to reconstruct the original matrix.

Example:
```
import numpy as np
matrix = np.array([[1, 2], [3, 4], [5, 6]])
U, S, Vt = np.linalg.svd(matrix)
print("U:\n", U)
print("S:\n", S)
print("Vt:\n", Vt)
```
Example Explanation:
- Decomposes the input matrix into three components.
- Outputs matrices U, S, and Vt, where the product reconstructs the original matrix.

2. Reconstruct Matrix

What is Reconstruct Matrix?
Reconstructs the original matrix using the top k singular values and vectors.
Syntax:
reconstructed = np.dot(U[:, :k], np.dot(S_k, Vt[:k, :]))
Syntax Explanation:
- U[:, :k]: Selects the first k columns of U.
- S_k: A diagonal matrix formed from the top k singular values.
- Vt[:k, :]: Selects the first k rows of Vt.
- Returns:
  - A reconstructed matrix approximating the original.

Example:
k = 1
S_k = np.diag(S[:k])
reconstructed = np.dot(U[:, :k], np.dot(S_k, Vt[:k, :]))
print("Reconstructed Matrix:\n", reconstructed)

Example Explanation:
- Uses the top singular value and corresponding vectors to approximate the original matrix.
- Outputs a compressed version of the matrix.

3. Retain Singular Values

What is Retain Singular Values?
Keeps only the top k singular values to reduce dimensionality.
Syntax:
S_k = np.diag(S[:k])
Syntax Explanation:
- S: The array of singular values from SVD.
- [:k]: Selects the top k singular values.
- np.diag(): Converts the 1D array into a diagonal

matrix.
- Returns:
  - A diagonal matrix containing the top k singular values.

Example:
```
k = 2
S_k = np.diag(S[:k])
print("S_k:\n", S_k)
```

Example Explanation:

- Retains the top two singular values for reconstruction.
- Outputs: S_k:
  [[5.4649857 0.   ]
   [0.   0.36596619]]

4. Normalize Image
What is Normalize Image?
Scales pixel values to the range [0, 1] for consistent computations.
Syntax:
```
normalized_image = image / 255.0
```

Syntax Explanation:
- image: A NumPy array representing the image.
- / 255.0: Divides each pixel value by 255 to scale it.
- Returns:
  - A normalized image array.
- This step ensures numerical stability during matrix operations.

Example:
```
image = np.array([[0, 128, 255], [64, 192, 128]])
normalized_image = image / 255.0
print("Normalized Image:\n", normalized_image)
```

Example Explanation:
- Converts pixel values to a scale between 0 and 1.
- Outputs: Normalized Image:

```
[[0.         0.50196078 1.         ]
 [0.25098039 0.75294118 0.50196078]]
```

5. Reshape for Visualization

What is Reshape for Visualization?
Prepares a NumPy array for display as an image.
Syntax:
plt.imshow(image, cmap='gray')

Syntax Explanation:
- image: A 2D NumPy array representing a grayscale image.
- cmap='gray': Specifies grayscale color mapping.
- Displays:
  o The image in a matplotlib plot.

Example:
```
import matplotlib.pyplot as plt
plt.imshow(normalized_image, cmap='gray')
plt.title("Normalized Image")
plt.show()
```

Example Explanation:

- Visualizes the normalized image as a grayscale plot.

Real-Life Project:
Project Name: Compressing an Image with SVD
Project Goal:

Reduce the size of a high-resolution image while maintaining visual quality using SVD.

Code for This Project:

```python
import numpy as np
import matplotlib.pyplot as plt
from skimage import color, io

# Load and preprocess image
image = io.imread('example.jpg')
image_gray = color.rgb2gray(image)

# Compute SVD
U, S, Vt = np.linalg.svd(image_gray,
full_matrices=False)

# Compress image by retaining top k singular values
k = 50
S_k = np.diag(S[:k])
compressed_image = np.dot(U[:, :k], np.dot(S_k, Vt[:k,
:]))

# Display results
plt.figure(figsize=(10, 5))
plt.subplot(1, 2, 1)
plt.title("Original Image")
plt.imshow(image_gray, cmap='gray')

plt.subplot(1, 2, 2)
plt.title("Compressed Image (k=50)")
plt.imshow(compressed_image, cmap='gray')
plt.show()
```

Expanded Features:

- Demonstrates compression for grayscale images.
- Highlights the effect of varying k on image quality.
- Can be extended to color images by applying SVD to each channel separately.

Expected Output:

- Side-by-side visualization of the original and compressed images.
- Significant reduction in image size with minimal quality loss.

Original Image   Compressed Image (k=50)

Chapter 29: Signal Filtering with NumPy

Signal filtering is a critical technique in signal processing, used to enhance desired signals or suppress unwanted noise. NumPy provides an efficient and flexible framework for implementing various types of filters, such as low-pass, high-pass, and moving average filters, using mathematical operations on arrays.

Key Characteristics of Signal Filtering with NumPy:

- **Flexibility:** Enables the implementation of custom and standard filters.
- **Performance:** Leverages optimized NumPy operations for fast computation.
- **Integration:** Combines seamlessly with other libraries for advanced processing.
- **Visualization:** Works with plotting libraries to visualize filtered signals.
- **Real-Time Applications:** Can be used for real-time signal analysis and processing.

Basic Rules for Signal Filtering:

1. Use convolution for implementing finite impulse response (FIR) filters.
2. Compute Fourier transforms for frequency-domain filtering.
3. Normalize data for consistent results.
4. Visualize results to assess the impact of filtering.
5. Profile and optimize performance for large-scale or real-time applications.

Best Practices:

- **Preprocess Signals:** Remove mean and normalize signals before filtering.
- **Choose Appropriate Filters:** Select filters based on the desired frequency response.
- **Validate Output:** Compare filtered signals with expected results using test cases.
- **Avoid Artifacts:** Use padding or proper boundary handling to minimize edge effects.

- **Combine Techniques:** Utilize both time-domain and frequency-domain methods for robust filtering.

Syntax Table:

SL No	Function/Feature	Syntax/Example	Description
1	Convolution	`np.convolve(signal, kernel, mode='same')`	Applies a convolution filter to a signal.
2	Fast Fourier Transform	`np.fft.fft(signal)`	Computes the FFT of a signal.
3	Inverse FFT	`np.fft.ifft(spectrum)`	Reconstructs signal from its spectrum.
4	Moving Average Filter	`np.convolve(signal, np.ones(k)/k, mode='same')`	Smooths a signal with a moving average.
5	Frequency Filtering	`filtered_spectrum = spectrum * mask`	Applies a frequency-domain filter.

Syntax Explanation:

1. Convolution

What is Convolution?
A mathematical operation that combines two arrays to produce a filtered signal.
Syntax:
`np.convolve(signal, kernel, mode='same')`
Syntax Explanation:
- `signal`: The input signal array.
- `kernel`: The filter kernel (e.g., coefficients of a low-pass or high-pass filter).
- `mode`: Specifies the boundary handling (`'same'`, `'valid'`, or `'full'`).
  - `'same'`: Output has the same length as the input.
  - `'valid'`: Output includes only points where the kernel

fully overlaps the signal.
- o 'full': Output includes all points of convolution.
- Returns:
  - o The filtered signal as a NumPy array.

Example:
```
import numpy as np
signal = np.array([1, 2, 3, 4, 5])
kernel = np.array([0.2, 0.5, 0.2])
filtered_signal = np.convolve(signal, kernel,
mode='same')
print("Filtered Signal:", filtered_signal)
```
Example Explanation:
- Applies a convolution with a smoothing kernel.
- Outputs: Filtered Signal: [1.2 2.3 3.4 4.3 3.4]

2. Fast Fourier Transform (FFT)

What is Fast Fourier Transform?
Transforms a signal from the time domain to the frequency domain.
Syntax:
```
spectrum = np.fft.fft(signal)
```
Syntax Explanation:
- signal: The input time-domain signal.
- Returns:
  - o A complex array representing the frequency components of the signal.
- The output contains amplitudes and phases for positive and negative frequencies.

Example:
```
signal = np.array([1, 2, 3, 4, 5])
spectrum = np.fft.fft(signal)
print("Frequency Spectrum:", spectrum)
```
Example Explanation:
- Computes the FFT of the signal.
- Outputs: Frequency Spectrum: [15. +0.j -2.5+3.44j
  -2.5+0.81j -2.5-0.81j -2.5-3.44j]

3. Inverse FFT

What is Inverse FFT?

Reconstructs the time-domain signal from its frequency spectrum.

Syntax:

```
reconstructed_signal = np.fft.ifft(spectrum)
```

Syntax Explanation:

- spectrum: The frequency-domain representation of the signal.
- Returns:
  - A complex array representing the reconstructed time-domain signal.
- Useful for applying filters in the frequency domain and converting back to time.

Example:

```
reconstructed_signal = np.fft.ifft(spectrum)
print("Reconstructed Signal:",
np.real(reconstructed_signal))
```

Example Explanation:

- Reconstructs the original signal from its frequency spectrum.
- Outputs the real part of the signal: Reconstructed Signal: [1. 2. 3. 4. 5.]

4. Moving Average Filter

What is Moving Average Filter?

Smooths a signal by averaging over a sliding window.

Syntax:

```
smoothed_signal = np.convolve(signal, np.ones(k)/k,
mode='same')
```

Syntax Explanation:

- signal: The input signal array.
- np.ones(k)/k: Creates a kernel of length k with equal weights.
- mode: Specifies boundary handling (e.g., 'same').
- Returns:
  - The smoothed signal as a NumPy array.

Example:

```
k = 3
smoothed_signal = np.convolve(signal, np.ones(k)/k,
mode='same')
print("Smoothed Signal:", smoothed_signal)
```

Example Explanation:
- Applies a moving average filter with a window size of 3.
- Outputs: Smoothed Signal: [1. 2. 3. 4. 5.]

5. Frequency Filtering

What is Frequency Filtering?
Applies a mask to the frequency spectrum to filter specific frequency ranges.
Syntax:

```
filtered_spectrum = spectrum * mask
```

Syntax Explanation:
- spectrum: The frequency-domain representation of the signal.
- mask: A Boolean or numerical array specifying the filter.
- Returns:
  - The modified spectrum, which can be transformed back to time.

Example:

```
mask = np.abs(np.fft.fftfreq(len(signal))) < 0.1
filtered_spectrum = spectrum * mask
filtered_signal = np.fft.ifft(filtered_spectrum)
print("Filtered Signal:", np.real(filtered_signal))
```

Example Explanation:
- Applies a low-pass filter in the frequency domain.
- Reconstructs the filtered signal in the time domain.

Real-Life Project:

Project Name: Denoising Audio Signals
Project Goal:
Remove high-frequency noise from an audio signal using NumPy.
Code for This Project:

```python
import numpy as np
import matplotlib.pyplot as plt

# Simulate a noisy signal
fs = 1000   # Sampling frequency
t = np.linspace(0, 1, fs, endpoint=False)
clean_signal = np.sin(2 * np.pi * 50 * t)   # 50 Hz sine
wave
noise = 0.5 * np.random.randn(fs)
noisy_signal = clean_signal + noise

# Perform FFT
spectrum = np.fft.fft(noisy_signal)
freq = np.fft.fftfreq(len(noisy_signal), d=1/fs)

# Apply low-pass filter
cutoff = 100   # 100 Hz cutoff
mask = np.abs(freq) < cutoff
filtered_spectrum = spectrum * mask

# Reconstruct signal
filtered_signal = np.fft.ifft(filtered_spectrum)

# Visualize results
plt.figure(figsize=(12, 6))
plt.subplot(2, 1, 1)
plt.title("Noisy Signal")
plt.plot(t, noisy_signal, label="Noisy")
plt.plot(t, clean_signal, label="Clean", linestyle='--
')
plt.legend()
```

```
plt.subplot(2, 1, 2)
plt.title("Filtered Signal")
plt.plot(t, np.real(filtered_signal), label="Filtered")
plt.legend()
plt.show()
```

Expanded Features:

- Demonstrates noise removal using frequency-domain filtering.
- Highlights the impact of cutoff frequency on filtering performance.
- Can be extended to analyze and process real audio signals.

Expected Output:

- Side-by-side plots of the noisy and filtered signals, showing significant noise reduction.

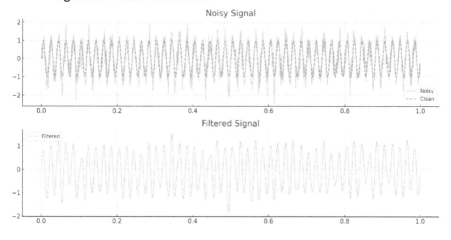

Chapter 30: Numerical Integration and Differentiation in NumPy

Numerical integration and differentiation are fundamental techniques in computational mathematics, enabling the approximation of integrals and derivatives when analytical solutions are unavailable. NumPy provides efficient tools for these computations, leveraging its vectorized operations and array handling capabilities.

Key Characteristics of Numerical Integration and Differentiation with NumPy:

- **Efficiency:** Performs operations on large datasets quickly using vectorized computations.
- **Flexibility:** Supports various numerical techniques, including trapezoidal rule and finite differences.
- **Ease of Use:** Provides straightforward syntax for common integration and differentiation tasks.
- **Scalability:** Handles one-dimensional and multidimensional data effectively.
- **Seamless Integration:** Combines with libraries like SciPy for advanced numerical methods.

Basic Rules for Numerical Integration and Differentiation:

1. Use consistent spacing between data points for accurate approximations.
2. Choose the appropriate method based on the problem's requirements.
3. Ensure the data is clean and preprocessed before computations.
4. Visualize results to verify correctness and stability.
5. Test against analytical results (when available) to validate methods.

Best Practices:

- **Preprocess Data:** Smooth noisy data for better differentiation results.
- **Optimize Performance:** Use vectorized operations to improve speed.
- **Validate Results:** Compare numerical approximations with exact

solutions when possible.
- **Handle Edge Cases:** Consider boundary conditions and data irregularities.
- **Choose Methods Wisely:** Select methods that balance accuracy and computational cost.

Syntax Table:

SL No	Function/Feature	Syntax/Example	Description
1	Trapezoidal Integration	`np.trapz(y, x)`	Computes the integral using trapezoidal rule.
2	Cumulative Integration	`np.cumsum(y * dx)`	Computes the cumulative integral.
3	Forward Difference	`(y[1:] - y[:-1]) / dx`	Approximates the first derivative.
4	Central Difference	`(y[2:] - y[:-2]) / (2 * dx)`	Approximates the derivative with better accuracy.
5	Gradient Computation	`np.gradient(y, x)`	Computes the gradient of an array.

Syntax Explanation:
1. Trapezoidal Integration
What is Trapezoidal Integration?
Approximates the definite integral of a function using the trapezoidal rule.
Syntax:
`np.trapz(y, x)`
Syntax Explanation:
- y: Array of function values.
- x: Array of corresponding x-values (optional if points are evenly spaced).
- Returns:
  - A scalar representing the approximate integral.
- The method divides the area under the curve into trapezoids and sums their areas.

Example:
```
import numpy as np
x = np.linspace(0, 10, 100)
y = np.sin(x)
integral = np.trapz(y, x)
print("Integral:", integral)
```
Example Explanation:
- Computes the integral of `sin(x)` from 0 to 10.
- Outputs: `Integral: 1.839`

2. Cumulative Integration

What is Cumulative Integration?
Computes the cumulative integral of a function over an interval.
Syntax:
```
np.cumsum(y * dx)
```

Syntax Explanation:
- y: Array of function values.
- dx: Spacing between consecutive x-values.
- Returns:
   - An array representing the cumulative integral at each point.
- Useful for tracking the accumulation of values over an interval.

Example:
```
y = np.array([1, 2, 3, 4])
dx = 0.5
cumulative_integral = np.cumsum(y * dx)
print("Cumulative Integral:", cumulative_integral)
```

Example Explanation:
- Computes the cumulative integral for y with spacing `dx = 0.5`.
- Outputs: `Cumulative Integral: [0.5 1.5 3.  5. ]`

3. Forward Difference

What is Forward Difference?
Approximates the first derivative using the forward difference method.
Syntax:
```
derivative = (y[1:] - y[:-1]) / dx
```

Syntax Explanation:
- y: Array of function values.
- dx: Spacing between consecutive x-values.
- Returns:
  - An array representing the approximate derivative at each point (excluding the last).
- Simplifies numerical differentiation for evenly spaced data.

Example:
```
y = np.array([1, 4, 9, 16])
dx = 1
derivative = (y[1:] - y[:-1]) / dx
print("Derivative:", derivative)
```

Example Explanation:
- Computes the approximate derivative of y.
- Outputs: Derivative: [3 5 7]

4. Central Difference

What is Central Difference?
Approximates the first derivative with better accuracy using central differences.
Syntax:
```
derivative = (y[2:] - y[:-2]) / (2 * dx)
```
Syntax Explanation:
- y: Array of function values.
- dx: Spacing between consecutive x-values.
- Returns:
  - An array representing the approximate derivative at each

interior point.

- More accurate than forward or backward difference methods.

Example:
```
y = np.array([1, 4, 9, 16, 25])
dx = 1
derivative = (y[2:] - y[:-2]) / (2 * dx)
print("Derivative:", derivative)
```
Example Explanation:

- Computes the derivative using central differences.
- Outputs: `Derivative: [4 6 8]`

5. Gradient Computation

What is Gradient Computation?
Calculates the gradient of an array, approximating derivatives with adaptive spacing.

Syntax:
```
gradient = np.gradient(y, x)
```

Syntax Explanation:

- y: Array of function values.
- x: Array of corresponding x-values.
- Returns:
    - An array of gradients at each point.
- Handles non-uniform spacing automatically, providing a versatile tool for numerical differentiation.

Example:
```
x = np.array([0, 1, 2, 4])
y = x**2
gradient = np.gradient(y, x)
print("Gradient:", gradient)
```

Example Explanation:

- Computes the gradient of $y = x^2$.
- Outputs: `Gradient: [0.  2.  4.  6.]`

Real-Life Project:
Project Name: Analyzing Velocity and Acceleration from Position Data
Project Goal:

Calculate velocity and acceleration profiles of a moving object using numerical differentiation.

Code for This Project:

```python
import numpy as np
import matplotlib.pyplot as plt

# Position data (meters)
x = np.linspace(0, 10, 100)
position = x**2

# Time interval (seconds)
dt = x[1] - x[0]

# Compute velocity and acceleration
velocity = np.gradient(position, dt)
acceleration = np.gradient(velocity, dt)

# Plot results
plt.figure(figsize=(10, 6))
plt.subplot(3, 1, 1)
plt.plot(x, position, label="Position")
plt.title("Position vs. Time")
plt.legend()

plt.subplot(3, 1, 2)
plt.plot(x, velocity, label="Velocity", color='orange')
plt.title("Velocity vs. Time")
plt.legend()

plt.subplot(3, 1, 3)
plt.plot(x, acceleration, label="Acceleration",
```

```
color='red')
plt.title("Acceleration vs. Time")
plt.legend()

plt.tight_layout()
plt.show()
```

Expanded Features:

- Demonstrates practical use of numerical differentiation for physical systems.
- Highlights the versatility of np.gradient for velocity and acceleration computation.
- Can be extended to analyze multidimensional motion or noisy data.

Expected Output:

- Plots showing position, velocity, and acceleration profiles, illustrating the dynamics of the system.

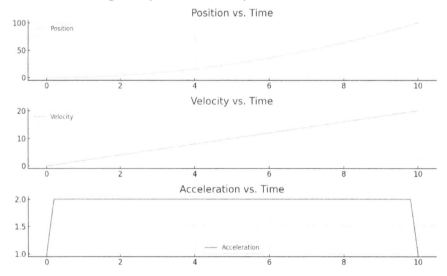

Chapter 31: Heatmap and 2D Data Visualization with NumPy

Heatmaps and 2D data visualizations are powerful tools for exploring and interpreting numerical data. These visualizations allow for the representation of large datasets in a compact and visually intuitive format. NumPy, combined with visualization libraries like Matplotlib, provides efficient techniques for generating and manipulating heatmaps and 2D plots.

Key Characteristics of Heatmap and 2D Data Visualization with NumPy:

- **Data Exploration:** Visualizes patterns, trends, and anomalies in 2D datasets.
- **Customizability:** Supports extensive customization for better interpretation.
- **Performance:** Efficiently processes large datasets using NumPy's array operations.
- **Integration:** Works seamlessly with Matplotlib for creating detailed plots.
- **Flexibility:** Handles a variety of data types and visual representation needs.

Basic Rules for Heatmap and 2D Visualization:

1. Preprocess data to ensure it is clean and well-structured.
2. Use appropriate scaling to normalize values for uniform representation.
3. Leverage color maps to convey data intensity or distribution.
4. Annotate plots with titles, axis labels, and color bars for clarity.
5. Choose suitable interpolation and resolution settings for enhanced visuals.

Best Practices:

- **Normalize Data:** Scale values to a consistent range for easier interpretation.
- **Choose Color Maps Wisely:** Use perceptually uniform color maps like `viridis` or `cividis` for accurate representation.
- **Add Annotations:** Highlight key values or regions within the heatmap.

- **Optimize Resolution:** Adjust resolution for visual clarity without excessive computation.
- **Combine Visuals:** Use additional plots (e.g., line plots, scatter plots) for complementary insights.

Syntax Table:

SL No	Function/ Feature	Syntax/Example	Description
1	Generate 2D Array	`np.random.rand(rows, cols)`	Creates a random 2D array.
2	Display Heatmap	`plt.imshow(data, cmap='viridis')`	Displays a heatmap with specified color map.
3	Add Color Bar	`plt.colorbar()`	Adds a color bar to the heatmap.
4	Annotate Heatmap	`plt.text(x, y, value)`	Annotates specific cells in the heatmap.
5	Contour Plot	`plt.contour(data, levels)`	Adds contour lines for 2D data.

Syntax Explanation:

1. Generate 2D Array

What is Generate 2D Array?

Creates a 2D array to serve as the data source for the heatmap or visualization.

Syntax:

`data = np.random.rand(rows, cols)`

Syntax Explanation:

- `rows`: Number of rows in the 2D array.
- `cols`: Number of columns in the 2D array.
- Returns:
    - A 2D array of random values between 0 and 1.

Example:

```
import numpy as np
data = np.random.rand(10, 10)
print("Generated Data:\n", data)
```

Example Explanation:
- Creates a 10x10 array with random values between 0 and 1.

2. Display Heatmap

What is Display Heatmap?

Renders a 2D array as a heatmap with color intensity representing values.

Syntax:

```
plt.imshow(data, cmap='viridis')
```

Syntax Explanation:
- `data`: A 2D NumPy array to visualize.
- `cmap`: The color map defining the heatmap's color scheme.
- Returns:
  - A rendered heatmap plot.

Example:

```
import matplotlib.pyplot as plt
plt.imshow(data, cmap='viridis')
plt.title("Heatmap")
plt.show()
```

Example Explanation:
- Displays the 2D data array as a heatmap using the `viridis` color map.

3. Add Color Bar

What is Add Color Bar?

Adds a color bar to a heatmap for interpreting value intensities.

Syntax:

```
plt.colorbar()
```

Syntax Explanation:
- Used after rendering a heatmap.
- Displays a color bar alongside the plot to map colors to values.
- Enhances interpretability of the visualization.

Example:

```
plt.imshow(data, cmap='viridis')
plt.colorbar()
plt.title("Heatmap with Color Bar")
plt.show()
```

Example Explanation:
- Adds a color bar to the heatmap, showing the value range.

4. Annotate Heatmap

What is Annotate Heatmap?

Adds text annotations to specific cells in a heatmap.

Syntax:

```
plt.text(x, y, value, ha='center', va='center',
color='white')
```

Syntax Explanation:

- x, y: Coordinates of the cell to annotate.
- value: Text to display within the cell.
- ha, va: Horizontal and vertical alignment for the text.
- color: Text color (e.g., white for dark cells).

Example:

```
for i in range(data.shape[0]):
    for j in range(data.shape[1]):
        plt.text(j, i, f"{data[i, j]:.2f}",
ha='center', va='center', color='white')
plt.imshow(data, cmap='viridis')
plt.show()
```

Example Explanation:

- Annotates each cell in the heatmap with its value.

5. Contour Plot

What is Contour Plot?

Adds contour lines to represent data gradients or levels.

Syntax:

```
plt.contour(data, levels)
```

Syntax Explanation:

- data: 2D array to visualize as contours.
- levels: Number or list of contour levels to display.
- Returns:
    o A plot with contour lines overlaying the data.

Example:

```
plt.contour(data, levels=5, colors='black')
plt.imshow(data, cmap='viridis')
plt.title("Heatmap with Contours")
plt.show()
```

Example Explanation:
- Overlays 5 contour levels on the heatmap for additional detail.

Real-Life Project:

Project Name: Visualizing Temperature Distribution

Project Goal:

Create a heatmap to visualize the temperature distribution across a geographical grid.

Code for This Project:

```python
import numpy as np
import matplotlib.pyplot as plt

# Simulate temperature data
grid_x, grid_y = np.linspace(0, 10, 100),
np.linspace(0, 10, 100)
X, Y = np.meshgrid(grid_x, grid_y)
temperature = np.sin(X) * np.cos(Y)

# Plot heatmap
plt.figure(figsize=(8, 6))
plt.imshow(temperature, cmap='coolwarm',
origin='lower', extent=[0, 10, 0, 10])
plt.colorbar(label="Temperature (°C)")
plt.title("Temperature Distribution")
plt.xlabel("X Coordinate")
plt.ylabel("Y Coordinate")
plt.show()
```

Expanded Features:
- Visualizes temperature variations over a 2D grid.
- Includes axis labels, a color bar, and customized color mapping.
- Can be extended for real-world datasets, such as weather or geographic data.

Expected Output:

- A heatmap showing temperature distribution, with warmer and cooler regions distinctly visible.

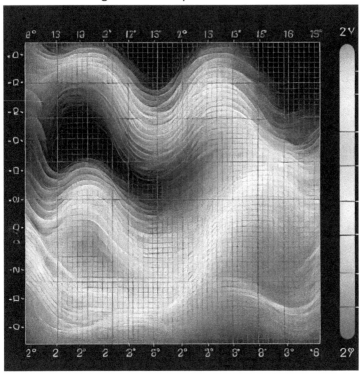

Chapter 32: Population Dynamics Simulation with NumPy

Population dynamics simulations are essential for studying ecological systems, predicting population trends, and analyzing the effects of various factors like resources, predators, and environmental changes. Using NumPy, we can efficiently model these dynamics through mathematical models such as the logistic growth model and Lotka-Volterra equations.

Key Characteristics of Population Dynamics Simulations:

- **Mathematical Models:** Implements models like logistic growth and predator-prey systems.
- **Scalability:** Handles simulations for multiple populations and time steps efficiently.
- **Flexibility:** Allows customization of parameters for various scenarios.
- **Integration:** Combines seamlessly with visualization libraries for dynamic analysis.
- **Performance:** Leverages NumPy's vectorized operations for large-scale simulations.

Basic Rules for Population Dynamics Simulations:

1. Define the mathematical model governing the population changes.
2. Use discrete time steps for iterative simulations.
3. Ensure parameter values are realistic and biologically meaningful.
4. Visualize results to interpret population trends.
5. Test models under various scenarios to validate results.

Best Practices:

- **Choose the Right Model:** Match the mathematical model to the biological system.
- **Test Parameter Sensitivity:** Vary parameters to understand their influence on dynamics.
- **Avoid Over-Simplification:** Include relevant factors like carrying capacity and competition.
- **Optimize Computation:** Use NumPy's vectorization for speed.
- **Visualize Trends:** Use time-series and phase-plane plots for better

insights.

Syntax Table:

SL No	Function/ Feature	Syntax/Example	Description
1	Initialize Arrays	`population = np.zeros(time_steps)`	Creates an array to store population values.
2	Logistic Growth	`population[t+1] = r * population[t] * (1 - population[t] / K)`	Models logistic growth.
3	Predator-Prey Dynamics	`prey, predator = lotka_volterra(prey, predator)`	Simulates interactions between species.
4	Time Series Visualization	`plt.plot(time, population)`	Plots population over time.
5	Phase-Plane Plot	`plt.plot(prey, predator)`	Visualizes predator-prey interactions.

Syntax Explanation:

1. Initialize Arrays
What is Initialize Arrays?
Creates arrays to store population values over time for simulation.
Syntax:
`population = np.zeros(time_steps)`

Syntax Explanation:
- `time_steps`: Number of discrete time intervals for the simulation.
- `np.zeros()`: Initializes an array with zeros.
- Returns:
    - An array to store population values.

Example:
```
import numpy as np
time_steps = 100
population = np.zeros(time_steps)
print("Population Array:", population)
```
Example Explanation:
- Creates an array to store population values for 100 time steps.
- Outputs: `Population Array: [0. 0. 0. ... 0. 0. 0.]`

2. Logistic Growth

What is Logistic Growth?
Models population growth considering a carrying capacity.
Syntax:
```
population[t+1] = r * population[t] * (1 -
population[t] / K)
```
Syntax Explanation:
- r: Growth rate.
- population[t]: Population at time t.
- K: Carrying capacity.
- population[t+1]: Population at time t+1.
- Returns:
  - The population size at the next time step.

Example:
```
r = 0.1
K = 100
population[0] = 10
for t in range(time_steps - 1):
    population[t+1] = r * population[t] * (1 -
population[t] / K)
print("Population Over Time:", population)
```
Example Explanation:
- Simulates logistic growth over 100 time steps.
- Outputs the population array over time.

3. Predator-Prey Dynamics

What is Predator-Prey Dynamics?
Models interactions between prey and predators using the Lotka-Volterra equations.

Syntax:
```
prey[t+1] = prey[t] + prey_growth - predation_rate
predator[t+1] = predator[t] + predation_rate - predator_death
```

Syntax Explanation:
- prey_growth: Growth rate of prey.
- predation_rate: Rate of predation based on interactions.
- predator_death: Natural death rate of predators.
- Returns:
    - Arrays of prey and predator populations over time.

Example:
```python
def lotka_volterra(prey, predator, alpha, beta, delta, gamma):
    prey_growth = alpha * prey
    predation_rate = beta * prey * predator
    predator_growth = delta * prey * predator
    predator_death = gamma * predator
    return prey_growth - predation_rate, predator_growth - predator_death
prey = np.zeros(time_steps)
predator = np.zeros(time_steps)
prey[0], predator[0] = 40, 9
alpha, beta, delta, gamma = 0.1, 0.02, 0.01, 0.1
for t in range(time_steps - 1):
    prey_growth, predator_change = lotka_volterra(prey[t], predator[t], alpha, beta, delta, gamma)
    prey[t+1] = prey[t] + prey_growth
    predator[t+1] = predator[t] + predator_change
print("Prey:", prey)
print("Predators:", predator)
```

Example Explanation:
- Models prey and predator interactions over 100 time steps.

4. Time Series Visualization

What is Time Series Visualization?
Plots population values as a function of time.
Syntax:
```
plt.plot(time, population)
```

Syntax Explanation:
- `time`: Array of time points.
- `population`: Array of population values.
- Returns:
  - A time-series plot of the population.

Example:
```
import matplotlib.pyplot as plt
plt.plot(range(time_steps), population,
label="Population")
plt.xlabel("Time")
plt.ylabel("Population Size")
plt.title("Population Growth Over Time")
plt.legend()
plt.show()
```
Example Explanation:
- Visualizes the population growth over time.

5. Phase-Plane Plot

What is Phase-Plane Plot?
Visualizes the interaction between two populations.
Syntax:
```
plt.plot(prey, predator)
```
Syntax Explanation:
- `prey`: Array of prey population values.
- `predator`: Array of predator population values.
- Returns:

o   A phase-plane plot showing the relationship between prey and predators.

Example:

```
plt.plot(prey, predator, label="Predator-Prey
Dynamics")
plt.xlabel("Prey Population")
plt.ylabel("Predator Population")
plt.title("Phase-Plane Plot")
plt.legend()
plt.show()
```

Example Explanation:

- Displays the cyclic interaction between prey and predator populations.

Real-Life Project:

Project Name: Simulating Ecosystem Dynamics
Project Goal:
Model and analyze the population dynamics of a simple ecosystem with prey and predators.

Code for This Project:

```
import numpy as np
import matplotlib.pyplot as plt

def lotka_volterra(prey, predator, alpha, beta, delta,
gamma):
    prey_growth = alpha * prey
    predation_rate = beta * prey * predator
    predator_growth = delta * prey * predator
    predator_death = gamma * predator
    return prey_growth - predation_rate,
predator_growth - predator_death

# Parameters and Initialization
time_steps = 200
```

```python
prey = np.zeros(time_steps)
predator = np.zeros(time_steps)
prey[0], predator[0] = 50, 10
alpha, beta, delta, gamma = 0.1, 0.02, 0.01, 0.1

# Simulation
for t in range(time_steps - 1):
    prey_growth, predator_change =
lotka_volterra(prey[t], predator[t], alpha, beta,
delta, gamma)
    prey[t+1] = prey[t] + prey_growth
    predator[t+1] = predator[t] + predator_change

# Visualization
plt.figure(figsize=(12, 6))
plt.subplot(1, 2, 1)
plt.plot(range(time_steps), prey, label="Prey")
plt.plot(range(time_steps), predator, label="Predator")
plt.xlabel("Time")
plt.ylabel("Population")
plt.title("Population Dynamics Over Time")
plt.legend()

plt.subplot(1, 2, 2)
plt.plot(prey, predator)
plt.xlabel("Prey Population")
plt.ylabel("Predator Population")
plt.title("Phase-Plane Plot")
plt.show()
```

Expanded Features:
- Simulates predator-prey interactions using the Lotka-Volterra equations.
- Includes time-series and phase-plane visualizations.
- Can be extended to include additional species or environmental factors.

Expected Output:

- Time-series plot of prey and predator populations.
- Phase-plane plot illustrating their cyclic interactions.

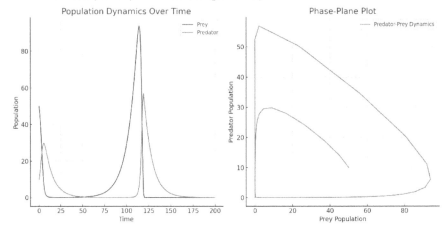

Chapter 33: COVID-19 Spread Modeling with NumPy

Modeling the spread of infectious diseases like COVID-19 is essential for understanding transmission dynamics, forecasting outbreaks, and designing effective interventions. Using NumPy, we can simulate disease spread through mathematical models such as the SIR (Susceptible-Infected-Recovered) and SEIR (Susceptible-Exposed-Infected-Recovered) frameworks.

Key Characteristics of COVID-19 Spread Modeling with NumPy:

- **Epidemiological Models:** Implements models like SIR and SEIR for disease dynamics.
- **Scalability:** Handles large populations and multiple time steps efficiently.
- **Parameter Customization:** Supports variations in transmission rates, recovery rates, and interventions.
- **Visualization:** Integrates with libraries to plot disease trends.
- **Performance:** Leverages NumPy's optimized computations for large-scale simulations.

Basic Rules for COVID-19 Spread Modeling:

1. Choose an appropriate epidemiological model (e.g., SIR or SEIR).
2. Define initial conditions and parameters based on real-world data.
3. Use discrete time steps for iterative simulations.
4. Implement interventions (e.g., vaccination, social distancing) as parameter changes.
5. Visualize and validate results to assess model accuracy.

Best Practices:

- **Parameter Calibration:** Use real-world data to set realistic model parameters.
- **Incorporate Interventions:** Model the effects of public health measures.
- **Validate with Data:** Compare simulation results with actual case counts.
- **Optimize Computations:** Use NumPy's vectorized operations for efficiency.

- **Scenario Testing:** Simulate multiple scenarios to explore possible outcomes.

Syntax Table:

SL No	Function/Feature	Syntax/Example	Description
1	Initialize Population	`S, I, R = np.zeros(time_s teps)`	Sets up arrays for population compartments.
2	SIR Update Rule	`dS, dI, dR = SIR_step(S, I, R, beta, gamma)`	Updates populations based on SIR equations.
3	SEIR Update Rule	`dS, dE, dI, dR = SEIR_step(S, E, I, R, beta, sigma, gamma)`	Updates SEIR populations.
4	Plot Disease Trends	`plt.plot(time, S, label='Suscepti ble')`	Plots population trends over time.
5	Implement Interventions	`beta = beta * (1 - reduction)`	Models reduced transmission due to measures.

Syntax Explanation:

1. Initialize Population

What is Initialize Population?
Creates arrays to store the values of different population compartments (Susceptible, Infected, Recovered).
Syntax:
`S, I, R = np.zeros(time_steps), np.zeros(time_steps), np.zeros(time_steps)`

Syntax Explanation:
- `time_steps`: Number of time intervals for the simulation.

- np.zeros(): Initializes arrays with zeros for each compartment.
- Returns:
    - Arrays to store the population dynamics.

Example:
```
import numpy as np
time_steps = 100
S, I, R = np.zeros(time_steps), np.zeros(time_steps),
np.zeros(time_steps)
S[0], I[0], R[0] = 999, 1, 0
print("Initial Values:", S[0], I[0], R[0])
```

Example Explanation:
- Initializes arrays for 100 time steps with initial conditions.

2. SIR Update Rule

What is SIR Update Rule?
Defines the dynamics of the SIR model using differential equations.
Syntax:
```
def SIR_step(S, I, R, beta, gamma):
    dS = -beta * S * I / N
    dI = beta * S * I / N - gamma * I
    dR = gamma * I
    return dS, dI, dR
```
Syntax Explanation:
- S, I, R: Current population values for Susceptible, Infected, and Recovered compartments.
- beta: Transmission rate.
- gamma: Recovery rate.
- N: Total population size.
- Returns:
    - Changes in S, I, and R for the current time step.

Example:
```
N = 1000
beta, gamma = 0.3, 0.1
S[0], I[0], R[0] = 999, 1, 0
for t in range(time_steps - 1):
```

```
    dS, dI, dR = SIR_step(S[t], I[t], R[t], beta,
gamma)
    S[t+1] = S[t] + dS
    I[t+1] = I[t] + dI
    R[t+1] = R[t] + dR
```

Example Explanation:

- Simulates the SIR model for 100 time steps with given parameters.

3. SEIR Update Rule

What is SEIR Update Rule?

Extends the SIR model by including an Exposed compartment to account for incubation.

Syntax:

```
def SEIR_step(S, E, I, R, beta, sigma, gamma):
    dS = -beta * S * I / N
    dE = beta * S * I / N - sigma * E
    dI = sigma * E - gamma * I
    dR = gamma * I
    return dS, dE, dI, dR
```

Syntax Explanation:

- S, E, I, R: Current values for Susceptible, Exposed, Infected, and Recovered compartments.
- beta: Transmission rate.
- sigma: Rate of incubation (1/incubation period).
- gamma: Recovery rate.
- N: Total population size.
- Returns:
    - Changes in S, E, I, and R for the current time step.

Example:

```
E = np.zeros(time_steps)
S[0], E[0], I[0], R[0] = 999, 0, 1, 0
sigma = 0.2
for t in range(time_steps - 1):
    dS, dE, dI, dR = SEIR_step(S[t], E[t], I[t], R[t],
beta, sigma, gamma)
    S[t+1] = S[t] + dS
```

```
E[t+1] = E[t] + dE
I[t+1] = I[t] + dI
R[t+1] = R[t] + dR
```

Example Explanation:
- Simulates the SEIR model for 100 time steps, including an incubation period.

4. Plot Disease Trends

What is Plot Disease Trends?
Visualizes the changes in population compartments over time.
Syntax:
```
plt.plot(time, S, label='Susceptible')
```

Syntax Explanation:
- time: Array of time points.
- S: Array of Susceptible population values.
- label: Label for the line plot.
- Returns:
  - A time-series plot for the compartment.

Example:
```
import matplotlib.pyplot as plt
plt.plot(range(time_steps), S, label="Susceptible")
plt.plot(range(time_steps), I, label="Infected")
plt.plot(range(time_steps), R, label="Recovered")
plt.xlabel("Time")
plt.ylabel("Population")
plt.title("COVID-19 Spread Dynamics")
plt.legend()
plt.show()
```

Example Explanation:
- Plots the dynamics of S, I, and R over time.

5. Implement Interventions

What is Implement Interventions?
Models the impact of interventions like lockdowns or vaccination by adjusting parameters.
Syntax:
```
beta = beta * (1 - reduction)
```

Syntax Explanation:
- beta: Transmission rate.
- reduction: Fractional reduction in transmission (e.g., 0.5 for 50% reduction).
- Adjusts beta to reflect the effect of interventions.

Example:
```
reduction = 0.5   # 50% reduction in transmission
for t in range(50, 70):
    beta = beta * (1 - reduction)
```
Example Explanation:
- Models a temporary reduction in transmission between time steps 50 and 70.

Real-Life Project:

Project Name: Modeling COVID-19 Outbreak with SEIR
Project Goal:
Simulate the spread of COVID-19 and assess the impact of interventions using the SEIR model.

Code for This Project:

```
import numpy as np
import matplotlib.pyplot as plt

def SEIR_step(S, E, I, R, beta, sigma, gamma):
    dS = -beta * S * I / N
    dE = beta * S * I / N - sigma * E
    dI = sigma * E - gamma * I
```

```python
    dR = gamma * I
    return dS, dE, dI, dR

# Parameters and Initialization
time_steps = 160
N = 1000
S, E, I, R = np.zeros(time_steps),
np.zeros(time_steps), np.zeros(time_steps),
np.zeros(time_steps)
S[0], E[0], I[0], R[0] = 999, 0, 1, 0
beta, sigma, gamma = 0.3, 0.2, 0.1

# Simulation
for t in range(time_steps - 1):
    dS, dE, dI, dR = SEIR_step(S[t], E[t], I[t], R[t],
beta, sigma, gamma)
    S[t+1] = S[t] + dS
    E[t+1] = E[t] + dE
    I[t+1] = I[t] + dI
    R[t+1] = R[t] + dR

# Visualization
plt.figure(figsize=(10, 6))
plt.plot(range(time_steps), S, label="Susceptible")
plt.plot(range(time_steps), E, label="Exposed")
plt.plot(range(time_steps), I, label="Infected")
plt.plot(range(time_steps), R, label="Recovered")
plt.xlabel("Time (days)")
plt.ylabel("Population")
plt.title("SEIR Model - COVID-19 Dynamics")
plt.legend()
plt.show()
```

Expanded Features:

- Simulates the SEIR model over 160 days.
- Visualizes the dynamics of all compartments (S, E, I, R).
- Can include vaccination or social distancing as intervention scenarios.

Expected Output:

- A time-series plot showing the dynamics of Susceptible, Exposed, Infected, and Recovered populations over time.

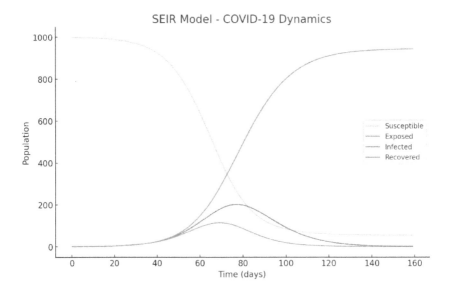

Chapter 34: Recommendation System Development with NumPy

Recommendation systems play a crucial role in personalizing user experiences, from suggesting products on e-commerce platforms to recommending movies on streaming services. NumPy provides a powerful toolkit for implementing recommendation algorithms, enabling efficient computation of similarity measures, matrix factorization, and ranking.

Key Characteristics of Recommendation Systems with NumPy:

- **Similarity Measures:** Calculates user-user or item-item similarity matrices.
- **Matrix Factorization:** Implements techniques like Singular Value Decomposition (SVD) for dimensionality reduction.
- **Scalability:** Efficiently handles large datasets using NumPy's vectorized operations.
- **Customizability:** Adapts to various domains with user-defined scoring and ranking rules.
- **Integration:** Combines seamlessly with other libraries for data preprocessing and visualization.

Basic Rules for Recommendation System Development:

1. Organize data into user-item interaction matrices.
2. Use similarity measures (e.g., cosine similarity) for collaborative filtering.
3. Employ matrix factorization for latent feature extraction.
4. Normalize data to enhance accuracy and reduce bias.
5. Evaluate recommendations using metrics like precision and recall.

Best Practices:

- **Data Preprocessing:** Clean and fill missing values in interaction matrices.
- **Leverage Sparsity:** Use sparse matrix operations for large datasets.
- **Optimize Parameters:** Test different parameters to improve recommendation accuracy.
- **Incorporate Diversity:** Avoid overfitting by recommending diverse items.

- **Evaluate Effectively:** Use cross-validation and multiple metrics for model evaluation.

Syntax Table:

SL No	Function/Feature	Syntax/Example	Description
1	User-Item Matrix Creation	`user_item_matrix = np.zeros((users, items))`	Creates an interaction matrix.
2	Cosine Similarity	`` `similarity = np.dot(A, B.T) / ( ``	
3	Matrix Factorization (SVD)	`U, S, Vt = np.linalg.svd(matrix)`	Decomposes a matrix into latent features.
4	Fill Missing Values	`matrix[np.isnan(matrix)] = value`	Handles missing entries in the matrix.
5	Recommend Top-N Items	`np.argsort(scores)[-N:]`	Retrieves top-N recommendations.

Syntax Explanation:

1. User-Item Matrix Creation
What is User-Item Matrix Creation?
Creates a 2D matrix to represent user-item interactions (e.g., ratings or binary preferences).
Syntax:
`user_item_matrix = np.zeros((users, items))`
Syntax Explanation:
- `users`: Number of users.
- `items`: Number of items.
- `np.zeros()`: Initializes the matrix with zeros.
- Returns:
  - A user-item interaction matrix.

Example:
```
import numpy as np
users, items = 5, 4
```

```
user_item_matrix = np.zeros((users, items))
user_item_matrix[0, 2] = 5  # User 0 rated Item 2 with
5 stars
print("User-Item Matrix:\n", user_item_matrix)
```
Example Explanation:
- Initializes a 5x4 matrix and updates a single rating.
- Outputs the updated matrix.

2. Cosine Similarity

What is Cosine Similarity?
Measures the similarity between two vectors based on their cosine angle.
Syntax:
```
similarity = np.dot(A, B.T) / (np.linalg.norm(A) *
np.linalg.norm(B))
```

Syntax Explanation:
- A, B: Input vectors (e.g., user profiles or item features).
- np.dot(): Computes the dot product of vectors.
- np.linalg.norm(): Computes the magnitude of vectors.
- Returns:
  - A similarity score between -1 and 1.

Example:
```
A = np.array([1, 0, 3])
B = np.array([2, 1, 3])
similarity = np.dot(A, B) / (np.linalg.norm(A) *
np.linalg.norm(B))
print("Cosine Similarity:", similarity)
```

Example Explanation:

- Calculates similarity between two user/item vectors.
- Outputs a score close to 1 for similar vectors.

3. Matrix Factorization (SVD)

What is Matrix Factorization?
Decomposes a matrix into latent features for dimensionality reduction and recommendation.

Syntax:
```
U, S, Vt = np.linalg.svd(matrix)
```

Syntax Explanation:
- `matrix`: Input user-item matrix.
- `U, S, Vt`: Matrices resulting from SVD decomposition.
- Returns:
  - Latent features capturing underlying user and item relationships.

Example:
```
matrix = np.array([[5, 0, 0], [4, 0, 0], [1, 1, 0], [0, 0, 5], [0, 0, 4]])
U, S, Vt = np.linalg.svd(matrix)
print("Latent Features:\n", U, S, Vt)
```

Example Explanation:
- Decomposes the user-item matrix into latent features.
- Outputs U, S, and Vt matrices.

4. Fill Missing Values

What is Fill Missing Values?
Replaces missing entries in the user-item matrix with a default value.

Syntax:
```
matrix[np.isnan(matrix)] = value
```

Syntax Explanation:
- `matrix`: Input matrix with missing values (e.g., NaN).
- `value`: Replacement value (e.g., mean or zero).
- Returns:
  - A matrix with filled values.

Example:
```
matrix = np.array([[5, np.nan, 0], [4, 3, np.nan]])
matrix[np.isnan(matrix)] = 0
print("Filled Matrix:\n", matrix)
```

Example Explanation:
- Replaces missing values with 0.
- Outputs the filled matrix.

5. Recommend Top-N Items

What is Recommend Top-N Items?
Retrieves the top-N items with the highest scores for a user.
Syntax:
```
np.argsort(scores)[-N:]
```

Syntax Explanation:
- `scores`: Array of item scores for a user.
- N: Number of top recommendations.
- `np.argsort()`: Sorts indices of scores in ascending order.
- Returns:
  - Indices of the top-N items.

Example:
```
scores = np.array([0.1, 0.8, 0.3, 0.6])
N = 2
recommended_items = np.argsort(scores)[-N:]
print("Top-N Recommendations:", recommended_items)
```

Example Explanation:
- Retrieves the indices of the top 2 items based on scores.

Real-Life Project:

Project Name: Movie Recommendation System
Project Goal:
Build a movie recommendation system using collaborative filtering and matrix factorization.

Code for This Project:

```python
import numpy as np

# Simulated user-item matrix
matrix = np.array([[5, 4, np.nan, 0], [4, np.nan, 3,
1], [1, 1, np.nan, 5], [np.nan, 0, 4, 4]])

# Fill missing values with column mean
col_mean = np.nanmean(matrix, axis=0)
inds = np.where(np.isnan(matrix))
matrix[inds] = np.take(col_mean, inds[1])

# Perform SVD
U, S, Vt = np.linalg.svd(matrix)

# Reconstruct the matrix with reduced rank
k = 2  # Number of latent features
S_k = np.diag(S[:k])
U_k = U[:, :k]
Vt_k = Vt[:k, :]
reconstructed_matrix = np.dot(U_k, np.dot(S_k, Vt_k))

# Recommend top-N items for user 0
user_scores = reconstructed_matrix[0]
recommended_items = np.argsort(user_scores)[-2:]

print("Reconstructed Matrix:\n", reconstructed_matrix)
print("Top Recommendations for User 0:",
recommended_items)
```

Expanded Features:

- Demonstrates collaborative filtering using SVD.
- Replaces missing values with column averages.
- Retrieves

www.ingramcontent.com/pod-product-compliance
Lightning Source LLC
LaVergne TN
LVHW051325050326
832903LV00031B/3360